Soldering
for
Jewellers

Rebecca Skeels

Soldering for Jewellers

Rebecca Skeels

THE CROWOOD PRESS

First published in 2017 by
The Crowood Press Ltd
Ramsbury, Marlborough
Wiltshire SN8 2HR
www.crowood.com

British Library Cataloguing-in-Publication Data

A catalogue record for this book is available from the British Library.

ISBN 978 1 78500 274 8

Acknowledgements
Special thanks to Paul Kenny for all his support, checking, patience, ideas, photography and advice. Andrew Wilgress and H.S. Walsh for supplying many of the images and enthusiasm.

Typeset by Kelly-Anne Levey
Printed and bound in India by Replika Press Pvt Ltd

CONTENTS

INTRODUCTION

Soldering is a process used to join two pieces of metal together by melting another metal with a slightly lower melting temperature between them. It is thought that soldering was developed to allow a larger variety of metals to be joined; it replaced the process of fusing and welding, in which jewellers used to melt two metals together. Fusing and welding is still appropriate for some techniques such as granulation and when working with metals such as steel. There is evidence of the use of soldering in jewellery thousands of years BC and we still use it today.

Soldering is one of the most utilized processes in jewellery making, however it is also one of the least highlighted processes when a piece is finished and ready to be displayed or worn. So it is unlikely to be discussed or even asked about unless you are learning. The main aim of soldering is to give work rigidity and strength, and it allows jewellers to push their ideas much further than making work without it. When beginners have practised soldering a few times they will start to use it in nearly everything they make and it becomes a familiar process to many jewellers and metalsmiths.

There are two types of soldering, one for the metals and solders that melt at low temperatures, such as pewter, lead and tin, known as soft soldering and one for the metals that melt at much higher temperatures such as copper, brass, silver, gold and platinum, known as hard soldering. Hard soldering is also known as brazing but most jewellers use the term 'soldering'.

Solder is made by mixing metal with other metal alloys. Metals mix a little like glass enamels; for example the colours stay separate instead of mixing like paint. Different metals have different sized molecules, so when they are mixed the little molecules fit in the gaps between the big molecules. Gold has much bigger molecules than silver, so when the big gold molecules are stacked the small silver molecules can hide in the gaps so much that there can be a higher percentage of silver and the gold stays as the dominant colour. The melting temperature of the solder is controlled by the amount of metal alloys added to the metal. With practice, it is worth keeping this in mind, as it will help you understand the process and take advantage of this knowledge. Most UK suppliers sell solders at set melting temperatures, but in the US and Japan it is worth asking the supplier for the melting temperature when you make your purchase. Remember that the melting temperature is when the metal melts, not the temperature at which the metal flows; this will be a higher temperature.

This book introduces soldering basics for jewellers. Basic techniques are explained to help you get started and allow you to explore soldering fully, giving yourself confidence to explore and challenge yourself further once you have undertaken a few experiments. The focus will be on silver soldering, which can be used for most non-ferrous metals such as silver. A similar process is used for other metals such as pewter,

OPPOSITE PAGE: **A typical working jeweller's bench.**

gold and platinum. It is advisable to try all the processes in this book in the order that they are written to enable you to have a full understanding of the advantages and disadvantages of each and to allow you to select the correct one for your own designs.

There are alternative joining processes such as rivets, tabs, setting, stitches, gluing, welding, fusing and so on. Rivets, tabs, setting and stitching can be used in conjunction with soldering and are ideal for including other materials in your work. For example, tabs can be soldered on to a ring and when the piece is finished they can be folded down over an object to hold it on to the ring

securely. This is the same principle as claw or rub over setting used for including stones on a piece. However, it is a good idea to think more broadly, to allow designs to be more unique.

Welding and fusing are usually used for metals that are not commonly used in jewellery, such as steel, aluminium and titanium, although they are coming back into fashion again. There are books focusing on these materials or you may want to start by attaching them to your work using the rivets, tabs or stitches as mentioned above. If you find yourself using titanium and steel more and more, you may want to look at the section on laser and PUK welding near the end of Chapter 1.

A variety of rivets.

Traditional welding is similar to soldering in that it uses a similar type of metal to help it join, but it is used more as a filler to bridge a gap or fuse two edges together. The problem with this is that the joint can be weak and messy, especially on smaller items such as jewellery. The filler metal can become porous as heat is only used in spot locations rather than over the whole piece, causing uneven cooling.

This book is here to motivate the beginner, with practice and play you will become confident fairly quickly. There are several projects to help you choose the best way to construct your own design and push the boundaries to produce unique ideas and pieces. You will find you are better at some processes than others, and with lots of practice you may adopt slight alternatives to some of the techniques that suit you and your designs better.

Jeweller's bench in the School of Craft and Design at the University for the Creative Arts in Farnham.

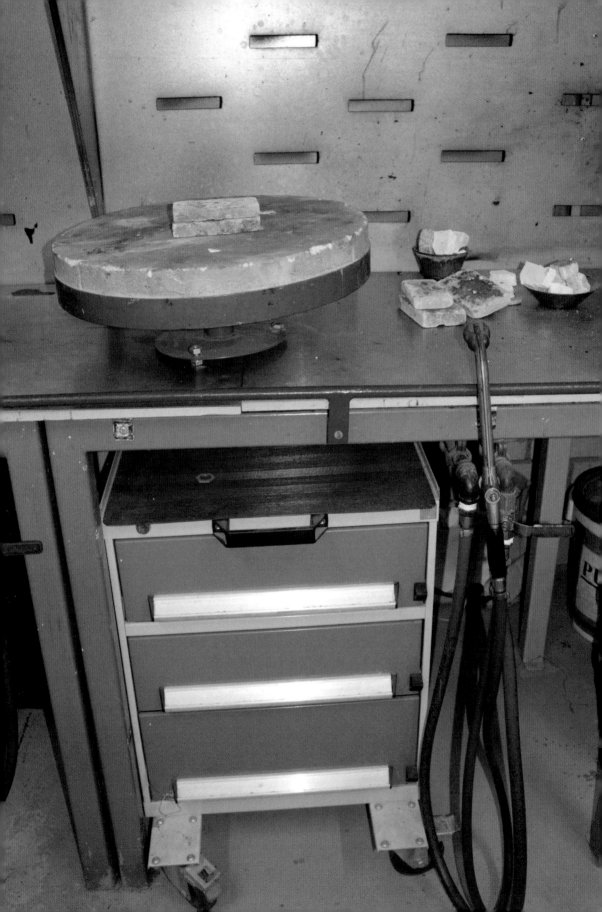

PREPARATION

It is important to plan the space you wish to use for designing and making jewellery. Most processes can take place in a relatively small area, enabling the set-up to be in a spare room or even part of a room. The priority when starting up is to think about health and safety and ensure you have organized and planned how and where to work safely. In this chapter health and safety issues will be discussed, followed by an explanation of the tools you will need for each step of the soldering process.

Safety goggles.

Health and Safety

It is essential to ensure that the environment in which you work and the processes you are undertaking will not cause harm or injury to yourself or any visitors you may have. It is advisable to make checks and put as many precautions in place as possible so you do not have to keep worrying every time you work.

When considering the environment, first and foremost ensure it is easy to use for yourself and the work you need to do. Make sure equipment is laid out to allow you to move between each process easily and that machines or equipment do not get damaged by adjacent activities. Also,

ensure walkways are clear and clutter-free, plus any liquids, gas and chemicals have safe storage spaces and you have a place for rubbish.

The soldering area needs to be in a space that has low light or can be shielded from light sources. When heating metal for many jewellery processes, such as annealing and soldering, it is easier to see the colour of the heated metal when there is no light reflecting off its surface. This is especially the case for white metals such as silver.

It is also good practice to understand what temperature the metal is at when you are heating it. For example, the first visible redness on silver is approximately 400°C, the dull red is around 650°C, and cherry red is around 760°C.

For your soldering area, it is advisable to protect the surfaces from heat and flames. Heat resistant board is fairly cheap and easy to cut to the size and shape of the work surface. Make sure that any heat reflective surfaces, bricks and blocks do not contain asbestos. You may also be

OPPOSITE PAGE: **Hearth area for larger scale soldering at the School of Craft and Design at the University for the Creative Arts in Farnham.**

Soldering area.

Safe place for lighters away from the soldering area.

using a lighter to ignite your torch. It is advisable to find alternative lighting methods, such as a striker or sparker, or alternatively have a place where you keep the lighter away from the soldering area. Get into the habit of returning the lighter to the storage place each time you use it to ensure it is not left where it can be accidently heated.

If you are just learning or starting out, you will likely be using small cans of gas but eventually you may wish to start using large gas bottles. When you have a large bottle on the premises, there are more regulations and requirements. For example, you will need to put a sign on the door of the building and room to let fire and rescue departments know a gas bottle is inside, so they can take necessary precautions in an emergency. Gas bottles need to be kept upright and in a well ventilated space where they cannot be knocked over and are ideally chained to a wall or sturdy fixture. Before you purchase your gas bottle, check the regulations with your gas supplier and the UKLPG, who are the trade association for the liquid petroleum gas industry in the UK.

Consider including a few pieces of safety equipment in your workspace in the unlikely situation that an accident does occur, such as a fire extinguisher

Sample of Area Risk Assessment
Please check the Heath and Safety Executive website for updated information
http://www.hse.gov.uk

AREA RISK ASSESSMENT

The 'Area Risk Assessment' is intended to provide an overall summary of the health and safety hazards and arrangements in each area. It should be read in conjunction with process and COSHH risk assessments.

		Room name / number	
Description of activities / use of area		Location	
		Maximum occupancy	
		AREA RISK RATING (With control measures)	□ Low
			□ Medium
			□ High
Summary of hazards (please tick✓)		□ Electricity □ Working at height □ Hazardous substances □ Moving machinery □ Lone working □ Use of hand tools □ Fire/explosion □ Manual handling □ Poor housekeeping	□ Dust / Fume □ Slips, trips & falls □ Screen Equipment □ □ □
Personal Protective Equipment (PPE) (The PPE highlighted is required for entry into the area, additional PPE may be required when carrying out processes)		□ Gloves □ Ear protection □ Stout or Enclosed footwear □ Safety footwear □ Respiratory protection	□ Overalls □ Eye protection □ Hard hat □ □
Who might be harmed?		□ Myself □ Visitors □ Contractors	□ Public □ Students □
List of relevant process risk assessments		□ soldering □ use of hand tools □ drilling □ enamelling and kiln work □ □ □ □ □ □	
Nearest emergency exit			
First aid contact details			
Any other information?			
Prepared by:			
Date:			

Sample of an area risk assessment form.

or fire blanket and a first aid or burns kit. There is a lot of information available online that will guide you when you are purchasing this type of equipment and your choice will depend on the size of the workshop and other activities that take place in the space.

If you open your work area up for open studios or to teach, it is highly recommended to write up potential risks in the form of a risk assessment. You may also be asked to provide a risk assessment when teaching or demonstrating elsewhere or exhibiting and hiring galleries. Create a simple form for yourself that you can fill in each time you introduce a new process or have bought new tools or equipment and keep the forms in your workspace so they are always to hand.

Things to consider when writing a risk assessment:

- **Title of activity or processes covered in assessment**
- **Hazards that can cause harm setting up, during and clearing up the activity**
- **Precautions put in place to lower or eliminate any risks of harm**
- **What to do in an emergency.**

Keep the assessment to one page so it is easy to read by you or by others and try not to imagine unlikely scenarios. The information to include is basic common sense. If this is an area you are really interested in and intend to start a business, you may wish to take a look at the Health and Safety Executive website or undertake a short course for more information on writing risk assessments.

Eye protection safety sticker.
(H.S. Walsh and Son Ltd)

Example of Coshh form.
Please check the Heath and Safety Executive website for updated information
http://www.hse.gov.uk.

COSHH Assessment Summary Product Details	
Product/Substance Name	
Description/Form	
Concentration(s) used	
Potential Hazards	
Exposure Limits	

Toxic | Gasses under pressure | Irritation | Flammable | Explosive | Harmful to environment | Oxidising | Respiratory, reproductive toxicity | Corrosive

Route of entry		Skin		Eyes		Inhalation		Ingestion	
R – Phrases (RISK PHRASES)									
S – Phrases (SAFETY PHRASES)									

Process Identification & Persons at Risk	
Intended Use / Operation	
Persons at Risk	

Personal Protective Clothing & Equipment	
Respiratory Protection	
Eye Protection	
Protective Clothing	
Other	

First Aid Measures	
Skin Contact	
Eye Contact	
Inhalation	
Ingestion	
In all cases of doubt or where symptoms persist seek immediate medical advice.	

Controls & Health Surveillance	
Control Measures	
Local Exhaust Ventilation	

Storage, Disposal & Emergency Action	
Handling & Storage	
Stability & Reactivity	
Spillage & Disposal	
Fire Fighting	

Assessment Details		
Name of Assessor:	Date:	
Date:	Signed off by:	

Sample of a COSHH form.

The best precautions to put in place when carrying out the soldering processes are:

- **To ensure you tie long hair, ties and scarves up and away from flames.**
- **Wear safety goggles or glasses to protect your eyes.**
- **Wear a leather or cotton apron to protect clothing from any hot items lodging in your clothes.**
- **Wear suitable shoes that fully cover your feet to ensure if anything hot does fall it will not make contact with your skin.**

Another form you should consider is the **control of substances hazardous to health, also known as** COSHH. These documents focus on substances rather than processes, and include dusts, gas, liquids and even solids such as metals. The easiest way to manage this area is to always ask for a materials safety data sheet when ordering any new substances or materials. These data sheets should contain all the information you need for a COSHH form. As with the risk assessments, keep the forms in the work area close to hand, so if there is an accident they can be taken to the doctors or hospital with you and the appropriate action can be taken swiftly to ensure there is limited damage to you and your health. Again, keep the form to one page so it is easy to read. You can find more information on the Health and Safety Executive website or there are short courses for more information on understanding this type of risk analysis if you are intending to start a business. At the very least, always read the data sheets for the substances you are using in and around your workspace. You are responsible for your own safety and the safety of others around you.

You must check your insurance details and discuss what you are using and doing with the company and landlord that insures the building and the contents where you are setting up your workspace. If you have visitors to your work area you will need public liability insurance to cover yourself in the unlikely event that you or a visitor has an accident. Many small businesses and individuals get good rates of insurance and discounts through memberships of organizations such as the a-n Artists Information Company and the Association for Contemporary Jewellery, both listed in the further information and suppliers section of this book.

Equipment

When purchasing equipment, it is best to start with the basics and build up as your interest grows and you know which items you use most often. The jewellery industry is extremely broad and has many different processes and techniques, so it is best to choose the technique that suits your designs and ideas rather than try to learn everything before you start.

The basic tools for soldering include a torch, a brick and tweezers and, of course, your apron, goggles and suitable shoes. All other tools and materials are for setting up and preparation of soldering, for cleaning up and finishing your piece afterwards. In this section you will be introduced to the basic tools and equipment. You will be introduced to more tools, tips and alternatives in the later chapters and projects.

Getting Everything Ready

To prepare for soldering, your metal and solder needs to be clean of any dirt and grease. Start by cleaning your hands; transferring dirt, grease or polish from your own hands on to the piece you are soldering is very easy as you need to handle your work regularly. Then set out to clean the joint; you can choose from various cleaning materials depending on the surface finish of which you are aiming.

All metal cleaning materials will be abrasive so bear in mind what effect you wish to achieve after you have soldered. For example, use a very fine abrasive for a shiny polished finish, as you will want to eliminate extra work later on. Many abrasive papers are available in a variety of grades, usually the higher the number the finer it is. Wet or dry paper is a popular choice for jewellers. It is called wet or dry so you can wash the metal particles out of it or use it wet to avoid it clogging up, making it efficient and long lasting. Pumice powder was traditionally used and is still popular with some jewellers; it is usually applied with a nylon bristle brush and a little water. More recently scourers have become more popular and different grades can be purchased but the standard domestic cleaning green scouring pad

A variety of abrasive rubber blocks.

Wet or dry paper. (H.S. Walsh and Son Ltd)

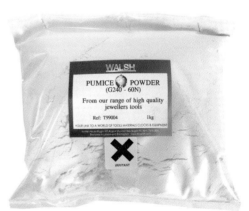

Pumice powder. (H.S. Walsh and Son Ltd)

Various scourers.

Nylon bristle brush. (H.S. Walsh and Son Ltd)

Borax cone and wrapper.

Borax dish. (H.S. Walsh and Son Ltd)

Borax cone in dish.

Flux brush. (H.S. Walsh and Son Ltd)

does the trick. Remember, you only need to clean the joint; you do not want to encourage the solder to flow anywhere else or change the surface of the metal that you intend to see when you have finished.

Once your work and solder is clean you will want to ensure it stays clean and the solder flows. Use a flux on the solder and the pieces you are connecting together. The most traditional flux for silver, copper, brass, gilding metal and gold is borax and is usually bought in a cone form and ground into a dish to create a milky paste. A brush is used to apply flux, with the best brushes made with natural hair and a plastic handle so they do not deteriorate or leave bristles on the work.

Holding the Work

To hold your work in place while it is being soldered it is easiest to lean one piece on top of another, relying on gravity to keep them in place. If the shape or form of the pieces means this is not possible then binding wire is the next most common material to use.

Binding wire is usually annealed steel wire covered with a layer of iron oxide to decrease the chances of it soldering to the work piece. Binding wire should be able to be easily wrapped

Binding wire. (H.S. Walsh and Son Ltd)

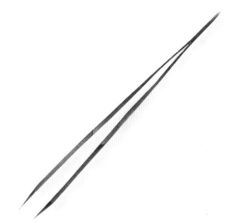

Steel tweezers. (H.S. Walsh and Son Ltd)

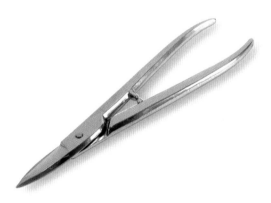

Tin snips. (H.S. Walsh and Son Ltd)

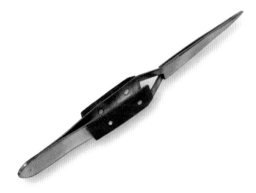

Reverse action tweezers for holding work. (H.S. Walsh and Son Ltd)

around your work to ensure it does not come apart when heated. For jewellery it is easier to use wire that is 0.8mm or thinner. The general rule is to use a thinner wire than the thickness of metal used in the piece you are making and not to wrap the work too tightly, so it does not become distorted. It is essential to remember to remove all binding wire from your piece before you pickle it as this can cause a chemical reaction in your pickle and plate your items in copper, *see* the cleaning up section of this chapter for more information on pickle. Some jewellers use binding wire a lot while others find it is best to avoid using it unless absolutely necessary. Finding alternative ways of holding work in place will be covered later as this is essential to the success of the soldering process.

You may already have some of the tools you need for setting up to solder, such as tweezers and tin snips. Tin snips are useful for cutting metal as well as allowing you to cut your solder into thin strips or small squares. It is advisable to have a pair of steel tweezers to work with when heating the work, picking it up and quenching it after you have soldered your piece. These are usually heavier steel and longer than standard tweezers to ensure the ends do not get damaged quickly and the heat does not travel along the tweezers when working in the heat. Remember, metal objects do not have to glow red to be hot,

Solder strip. (H.S. Walsh and Son Ltd)

Solder panel. (H.S. Walsh and Son Ltd)

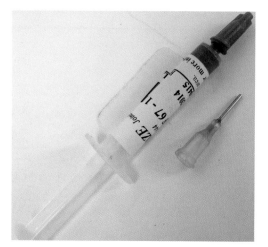

Solder paste. (H.S. Walsh and Son Ltd)

Solder wire. (H.S. Walsh and Son Ltd)

so be careful not to pick up your work before cooling it or pick the tweezers from the end you have had in the heat.

You may wish to have a standard pair of tweezers that you do not use when heating work, so they are not damaged and they allow you to pick up small solder pieces and put them in place. Reverse action tweezers are also extremely useful. These open when squeezed rather than the other way around, so they can be used to hold items in place while soldering. More on this later.

Solder

Solder can be bought in a variety of forms to enable you to solder different metals or a combination of metals. Silver solder is commonly used for silver, brass, copper and gilding metal, and can be purchased at a variety of melting temperatures to help you solder many times on to one piece. Gold solder also can be purchased with a variety of melting temperature points, as well as obtained in red, yellow or white gold. Gold and silver solders are available at various suppliers as traditional strips, panels and wires, as well as a paste or in a syringe.

Pewter can only be soldered with a pewter or tin solder. The melting temperature of pewter is much lower than the other metals and will melt easily. However, you may wish to experiment using pewter solder to solder other metals together. Do be warned though, pewter and aluminium can contaminate precious metals, even a small grain or bit of pewter or aluminium dust on silver will create a hole when heated. This can have disastrous consequences if not planned. Also, the lower flow temperature of the pewter solder will create a weaker bond more like glue, so do consider what you will use your piece for.

Heating

When the work is clean and fluxed, it is best to set the work up on a soldering brick. These are heat reflective blocks that stop the surfaces underneath them getting damaged, but also reflect the heat to aid the soldering process by keeping the metal hot. Traditionally, charcoal blocks were used and they are extremely good at reducing the oxygen in the atmosphere. Other bricks cannot provide this effect, although with the development of asbestos substitutes, soldering bricks are now cheaper, longer lasting and cleaner, and do a great job. Remember, do not use anything that contains asbestos.

In industrial and mass manufacturing processes, a kiln or furnace is used to heat the metal when soldering, however most jewellers working at a bench use a torch.

When starting out you may wish to purchase a gas torch that eliminates the need for large gas bottles or plumbing in new gas pipes for natural gas as well as setting up a compressed air system. Torch heads on a gas canister can now be purchased at extremely reasonable prices from

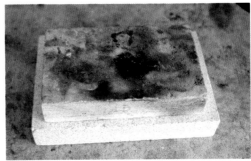

Soldering bricks, for reflecting heat back on to the work.

Soldering sheet to protect the surface of the bench or work surface.

Charcoal block for reflecting heat back on to the work. (H.S. Walsh and Son Ltd)

Torch and spare can of gas for small and medium sized work.

hardware stores and will be sufficient for most jewellery projects. There are various options for the torch head that screws to the can of gas. A jewellery torch head or a fine flame torch head will suit most jewellery tasks, but you may wish to have a larger head if you plan to make larger scale pieces.

Torch for smaller items and can be filled with lighter gas refills. (H.S. Walsh and Son Ltd)

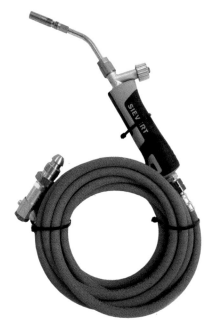

Jeweller's torch that uses bottled gas and needs no extra air source. (H.S. Walsh and Son Ltd)

Butane or butane propane mixed gas can be used. The mix is usually made so it can be used in very cold climates and the gas has an added odour so it is easier to detect if there is a leak. Both mixes work for standard room temperatures and are much safer and cleaner than natural gas. In recent years, crème brûlée torches have become popular, especially as they are used to fire metal clays. However, they tend not to be able to heat up very large items and will be unsuitable for most jewellery projects.

If you want a set up to do soldering regularly, propane can be bought in larger steel canisters, too and it is often called liquid propane gas or LPG. As mentioned in the Health and Safety section of this book, do check up to date regulations before purchasing and storing the gas. Propane canisters are easy to get refilled by a gas supplier or garage, enabling you to purchase the gas when you need it. Ensure you purchase appropriate connections from a recognized supplier and remember propane butane mix creates an odour to help the detection of any leaks.

Liquid propane gas bottle.

Close up of torch head, designed to allow air to be drawn in. (H.S. Walsh and Son Ltd)

Close up of torch head; the holes allow air to be drawn in.

In addition to the gas, the torch needs to provide air either by hoses plumbed in or by the torch head design that allows air to be drawn in from the atmosphere. The air supply allows the flame to go from a natural yellow to a sharp blue point. When soldering you will want a soft fluffy flame to dry out the flux and metal, then add a little air to create a pale blue sharper flame for soldering.

There are three common flame types:

- 'Reducing' is so named because it provides an oxygen reducing atmosphere with a deep blue cone centre with orange flecks. The yellow fluffy wiggly flame is great for warming up flux, drying out materials and annealing metal. Add a little air, keeping the flame bushy, to solder work.
- 'Neutral' flame has a sharper medium blue middle and orange tip; it has a balance of gas and air and will heat up the metal quicker than the reducing flame.
- 'Oxidizing' flame is sharp, thin and is best to use on metals that do not oxidize, such as platinum. This flame heats metal up fast and is most likely to cause fire scale on silver objects.

Cleaning Up

Avoid cleaning the work until all the soldering has been completed, as this will reduce the risk of seams opening and the creation of fire scale. When your pieces are soldered, you will need to remove the remaining flux and oxides. A 'pickle' is a solution that is most commonly used to clean the metal after soldering. It is essential to remove all flux residue as it will form a glass on the surface of the metal that will be hard to remove by sanding or filing. A glassy flux surface can damage tools and can result in surrounding metal being removed before the flux.

Slow cooker hot plate with Pyrex dish to hold pickle.

Mini pickle tank. (H.S. Walsh and Son Ltd)

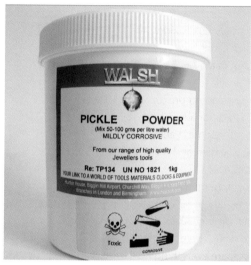

Safety pickle salts. (H.S. Walsh and Son Ltd)

Picklean salts. (H.S. Walsh and Son Ltd)

Bicarbonate of soda for neutralizing acid.

Safety mask to be worn when mixing chemicals.

Gloves to be worn when mixing safety pickles.

The process of metal pickling is acid dipping to remove flux, oxides, fire scale and fire stain. The pickle solution can be used cold but is usually kept in a pickle tank or more often a slow cooker. This allows the jeweller to warm it up, making the cleaning process much faster.

Traditionally pickle was made up of a 10 per cent sulphuric acid in water solution. However, it is easier and safer to purchase safety pickle salt from jewellery suppliers. If you are making a sulphuric acid solution remember to abide by any safety instructions on the data sheet and packaging. Always add acid to water, not water to acid. The easy way to remember is to always prepare everything first and leave the dangerous bit of adding the acid to last. While adding acid to water wear rubber gloves, apron and sensible shoes to ensure that no acid comes in contact with your skin. Work in a well ventilated area and mix the solution in a glass or highly glazed container and have some bicarbonate of soda to hand to neutralize the acid and clear up any spills. Disperse the acid by pouring slowly and do not pour it into one area of the container.

If you are using safety pickle or a sulphuric acid solution always use it in a well ventilated area and rinse work thoroughly after it has been taken out. Do not put hot work into the solution as it creates a variety of problems from splattering acid, distortion of the work piece caused by cooling differently across the piece, excessive fumes and it may even crack the work. Let the work cool first then quench it in a bowl or jar of water before placing it in the pickle.

ALTERNATIVE PICKLE SOLUTIONS IN AN EMERGENCY

If you need to pickle something, but are waiting for a delivery of safety pickle try leaving your work in vinegar or cola.
The acid content will dissolve the glassy flux.
Be sure to rinse thoroughly after use.

Rubber aprons and face shields to be worn when mixing acids and chemicals.

You may wish to have a pair of plastic, brass or copper tweezers when placing your jewellery into the pickle. Make sure you can pick the work up easily and without scratching the surfaces. Like the binding wire, steel tweezers can cause a chemical reaction in the pickle and plate items in copper; this is annoying and hard to remove if it is not intended. Leave your work in the pickle

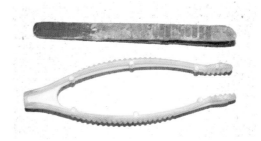

Wooden and plastic tweezers to be used with pickle solution.

Plastic tweezers to be used with pickle solution.

Brass tweezers to be used with pickle solution. (H.S. Walsh and Son Ltd)

Solder skull.

Solder ghost.

until all the oxides have gone and do not leave the work in for too long as it can break down the metal structure, leave solder porous and ruin the work that has been done. Rinse the tweezers and work thoroughly when it comes out of the pickle and wash your hands. Some jewellers use pumice powder with water to scrub the work and ensure all the pickle has been removed.

After the work has been pickled you can progress with smoothing large blemishes and remove excess solder with files and wet or dry paper, before putting the final desired finish on to the surface of the pieces. A remnant of solder is sometimes called a solder skull and needs to be removed completely as it will leave a yellow blotch on the work. Start by filing off the lump and follow by using wet or dry paper on a flat surface to ensure that a dip is not created in the metal. A solder ghost is the name used for a dip left after soldering. Overheating causes the zinc in the solder to eat into the silver, leaving a rough depression. Again, use wet or dry paper on a flat surface to remove as much of the dip as possible.

Keeping Up to Date

There is a continuous advancement in equipment within the jewellery industry, adding to the toolboxes of all jewellers and allowing the market to broaden with new options and ideas. It is important to keep up with changes and developments as some may be useful for the designs you wish to achieve. An example of developing technology has led to the invention of micro-welding systems and laser welders. The micro-welding systems weld metal together in a similar way to traditional welding. For example, the PUK welders made by Lampert in Germany use pulse arc welding. Laser welding is more precise and fuses the metal together utilizing a laser, creating a strong sturdy joint.

Currently, PUK and laser welding equipment is relatively expensive for a micro business or individual, but with each development it is becoming cheaper and more affordable. The laser welder and micro welding systems are used for various tasks within the jewellery industry as they have several advantages over soldering. For example, the heat is very localized so the work can be held in the hands, no flux is required, connections can be made near heat-sensitive stones, and multiple joints can be made without affecting each other. The disadvantages, as well as the high price, include the length of time the process takes and the loss of sharpness of corner and angled joints. The main current use is for the conservation and repair of jewellery in larger companies. However, silversmiths also find them useful for tacking work together before soldering long joints. It allows two large pieces to be held together securely without distorting or movement during heating of the work. Both welding processes also work extremely well on steel and titanium, allowing jewellers more options to achieve their design ideas with these materials.

Tools, alternative equipment and other materials such as fluxes, solders and metals will be discussed in more depth throughout this book. It is important to enjoy what you are learning and collect the information through reading, doing and looking at the images. A lot of the projects will use silver solder and copper as the main materials so the reader can see how the process works. These processes are used in the same way with silver, gold, brass and gilding metal. Try the processes out using copper, brass and gilding metal, as they are cheaper. This will allow you to explore a variety of ideas without the high cost of precious metals and your confidence will grow through practising. Chapter Nine will introduce soldering information for other metals, such as pewter, platinum and gold.

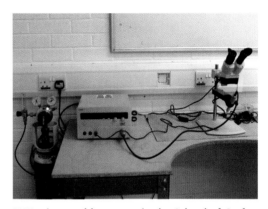

PUK micro welder set up in the School of Craft and Design at the University for the Creative Arts in Farnham.

Hallmarking

When you have a collection of jewellery you wish to sell, it is law in the UK to hallmark any metal items over a particular weight that are claimed to be silver, gold or platinum. For example, any silver item over 7.78g will need to be hallmarked. Information for hallmarking is obtained easily from assay offices in London, Birmingham, Edinburgh and Sheffield. The information is updated regularly so it is advisable to check with the assay office before you sell your work. Firstly, register with the assay office in order to register a maker's mark, which will last up to ten years. When sending work to be hallmarked, group as many items made from the same material together, as it is much cheaper to hallmark many items in one order rather than dealing with individual items.

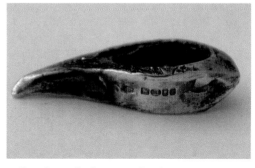

Hallmark on the bottom of a ring.

SETTING UP THE WORK TO BE SOLDERED

Spending time setting up work to be soldered is the most important part of the whole process. It will prevent mishaps, bad joints and worry. Areas and edges that are to be joined need to be clean, grease-free and fit together with no gaps. Consider each of the following steps each time you are preparing to solder. Remember, the aim is to create a joint strong enough for the application required.

The gap between the two edges that are to be soldered needs to be as small as possible. Hold the items together and up to the light; you should not be able to see any light through the two pieces.

The smaller the gap, the stronger your joint will be and it will be less visible for a variety of reasons. Firstly, the solder may be a slightly different shade from the metal despite how well you make a colour match, the solder and metal will wear differently as one will be softer than the other, and lastly the smaller the gap the less chance of porosity in the solder created by heating. The more the solder is heated to melting temperature the more it reacts with the atmosphere and creates very small holes.

Solder fills a gap with a capillary action; the molten liquid relaxes its surface tension allowing it to flow into the smallest openings. The solder will flow towards the hottest part of the metal, drawing it along the joint.

Next, ensure the area on the piece of work to be joined is clean. Firstly, clean your hands; if

you have any grease, polish or dirt on them you do not want it to be transferred on to the solder or metal and prohibit the solder from flowing.

Hold pieces up to a light and check there are no gaps along the joint to be soldered.

Wash your hands to keep your work, solder and flux clean.

OPPOSITE PAGE: **Close-up of honeycomb brick.**

Clean edges to be soldered, if using wet or dry on a flat edge, attach the wet or dry to a flat piece of wood.

The surfaces to be soldered need to be cleaned, even if the piece has just been pickled. A pickled surface does not take solder well.

The materials used to clean the joint will be abrasive so try not to mark the areas that are not to be soldered when doing this. There is no benefit from cleaning a larger area than required and encouraging the solder to flow where you do not want it or scratching and removing any textures previously applied. If you need a polished surface in an awkward space, sand and polish it up before you solder other parts in the way; this will eliminate extra work later on.

When cleaning the joint, try not to misshape the work or make a gap; you are only cleaning the surface. Many abrasive papers are available in various grades, usually the higher the number the finer it is, and the finer will probably suit your needs in this

Flux will only adhere to clean metal.

case. Wet or dry paper is a popular choice for jewellers. To keep the shapes on flat metal surfaces, stick the paper to another flat surface such as a piece of wood. For small work, **emery boards used for filing fingernails are really useful.**

Pumice powder is usually applied with a nylon bristled brush and a little water, but it is hard to keep to the areas required. More recently scourers have become more popular for cleaning metal as well as giving the metal a satin finish. Different grades of scourers can be purchased, however again this is hard to keep to the required areas.

When the area to be soldered is clean, you will want to ensure it stays that way and the solder flows. Paint flux on to the joint; this keeps it clean and stops it oxidizing while soldering, as well as reducing surface tension between solder and metal and helping it flow easily. If the flux or water balls up on the surface of the metal it means there is still grease present and you may need to clean it a little more.

Flux

Flux dissolves oxide residues and stops further oxides from forming, which means it keeps the metal clean and allows the solder to work. If an oxide layer is formed, the solder will only adhere to the surface like glue and is likely to come apart later. When learning to solder it is easy to overheat your metal, during which a copper oxide is formed in sterling silver, which can create a fire scale or fire stain. Fire stain can cause a purplish patchy pattern that has a less reflective surface. Flux also contains a wetting agent that encourages solder to flow along the seams, into the joints and into the structure of the metal, creating a strong bond.

It is possible to make flux, but in the UK there are plenty of suppliers that sell it ready made at a reasonable price without the problems of safety or purchasing the correct ingredients. It is also a

 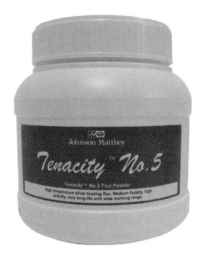 

LEFT: **Argo-tect was developed to protect silver from fire stain.**

MIDDLE: **Tenacity flux is usually used when soldering or brazing at temperatures below 850°C and where prolonged heating is required.**

RIGHT: **Easy-flo flux is used when soldering or brazing at temperatures below 750°C.**

(All images H.S. Walsh and Son Ltd)

material that you will not need to buy often as a small amount will go a long way. A flux will need to activate well below the melting temperature of the solder to protect the surfaces that are to be joined through the heating process. It also needs to survive just over the melting point and not burn away before the solder has flowed. You will find some fluxes that only work above a certain temperature, such as tenacity flux that activates above 600°C and can only be used with medium, hard or enamel solders.

The most traditional flux for silver, copper, brass, and gilding metal is borax. The borax bought from jewellery suppliers is usually a mix of borax, potassium carbonate and salt. Pure borax can become active a little late, be harder to remove and puff when heated. When purchasing borax in the UK it is usually bought in a cone form and ground into a dish to create a milky paste. Adding too much water can make it puff when heated, which in turn moves the work and the solder. If you have added too much water to the dish, drain some away or make up more paste. If you have

Firescoff ® has been developed to be used without other flux, to prevent fire stain and so there is no need for pickle solutions; it is easily applied by spraying on to the surfaces.

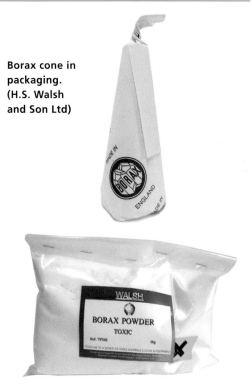

Borax cone in packaging. (H.S. Walsh and Son Ltd)

Borax powder is used for a wide variety of applications as well as soldering. (H.S. Walsh and Son Ltd)

LEFT: Auflux is a flux solution used for gold and silver soldering. (H.S. Walsh and Son Ltd)
RIGHT: Firescoff ® prevents fire stain and has no need for pickle solutions. (H.S. Walsh and Son Ltd)

added too much water and already applied it to your work, draw the water off slowly with a fluffy flame.

Borax can also be bought in a powder form that is commonly used for casting processes and is sprinkled into the metal to help it flow and to help remove dissolution product that

forms, creating a slag. Other fluxes can also be bought and these have different names depending on the supplier, such as auroflux or auflux, which are usually used for gold soldering, but can be used on silver, too. You may wish to also explore other flux solutions and powders, and especially in the USA there

Borax brushes. (H.S. Walsh and Son Ltd)

Pipe cleaners make ideal flux brushes.

are many more options, however borax will be suitable for all the soldering projects in this book.

Borax has some advantages for the beginner. It will take longer to burn away, allowing you to take your time getting the metal up to soldering temperature, and it allows it to be heated more than once if there is a need to stop the process and start again. Borax can also help hold pieces together and solder in place, almost gluing the solder to the surface during the heating process. Borax residues are fluoride based and can be dissolved in boiling water or pickle, allowing it to be easily removed when soldering is finished.

A brush is typically used to apply the borax and the best are made with natural hair and a plastic handle so they do not deteriorate. Alternative applicators can be used such as pipe cleaners or it can even be done by dipping the piece of work into the paste, but try to keep the borax and mixtures clean.

Binding Wire

The next stage is to secure your work while you solder it in place. Binding wire is common as it can cater for a variety of sizes, shapes and circumstances. The wire is usually annealed steel that can easily be wrapped around forms to ensure they do not come apart when heated. For jewellery the general rule is to use a thinner wire than the thickness of metal used in the piece you are making.

Binding wire tends to be wrapped around an object with a loop or kink placed every few centimetres along its length to make points where it can be tightened when setting up without re-wrapping it. The binding wire expands less than silver; the loops will also expand and contract a little when heated so will not mark the metal or pull it out of shape, but will hold enough not to allow the metal to move about. If

Only use binding wire if necessary. Prepare all the binding wire before you start to wrap the item.

the binding wire burns out, try using two pieces twisted together. This again gives it strength, but also the ability to contract and expand when heat is applied. It is advisable to prepare lengths of binding wire before starting to wrap them around the piece; this will help get them the right length and ensure all the loops are twisting in the same direction to tighten them.

Do not wire across gaps as it will pull the sides inwards as the metal relaxes and softens. Either use other methods of holding the work or hook the binding wire to the open edges. If you have binding wire crossing a seam, this may cause the solder to flow between the wire and piece of work. There is an iron oxide on binding wire to avoid this, but it is still possible so create a small bridge system with more binding wire to ensure it is not touching the metal at this point.

Use a bridging system if the binding wire crosses the joint that is being soldered.

Pin into the soldering surface to hold items in place.

Remember, as mentioned earlier, it is paramount that all binding wire that is not stainless steel is removed from your piece before you pickle it as it will plate your piece with copper. Most binding wire is made from mild steel as stainless steel is harder to wrap around small items. If binding wire causes more problems than it solves, try alternative methods of holding work in place, such as those mentioned in the next two paragraphs, or using the tools in the tool making section of this chapter.

Pins can also hold work in place. Stainless steel pins are cheap and ideal for pushing into soldering bricks, charcoal blocks or plaster.

Make small 'stitches' in the sheet to keep the metal in the right place.

They can also be strategically placed to stop work rolling, bending or moving. Be careful not to be too harsh when pushing them into place, as it is easy to break or crack a brittle soldering surface.

A practised engraver may also wish to use stitches to hold work together. These are small scrapings of metal that are taken from the surface of one piece being soldered to hold the other piece that is being soldered in place. This is extremely effective and traditionally used in box making, but has the disadvantage that there may be marks left where the scrapings have been made. Think carefully before using them and consider the whole design so they can be placed in an area that will not be seen. Laser and PUK welders are also used when making larger scale silver and gold work to join pieces at strategic points and hold them together while being soldered.

Heating Surfaces

When the work is clean, fluxed and bound, it is ready to be heated. There are various options of what to sit the work on. Most jewellers place work on to heat reflective blocks that stop the surfaces underneath them getting damaged. The blocks also reflect the heat to aid the soldering process by keeping the metal hot. The blocks are used for a variety of applications so are usually the base of the soldering area even if alternative options are required for some more complicated processes. Heat reflective blocks, bricks and sheets can be purchased from jewellery tool suppliers. Ceramicists may have a stock of kiln bricks that are no longer required. These are ideal to cut, pin into or carve if need be and can be cleaned easily by rubbing two together.

Charcoal blocks are extremely good as they can easily be shaped or pins can be pushed into

LEFT: **Supablox soldering brick.** MIDDLE: **Vermiculux soldering brick. (H.S. Walsh and Son Ltd)**
RIGHT: **Kiln brick. (All images H.S. Walsh and Son Ltd)**

Charcoal block for reflecting heat back on to the work. (H.S. Walsh and Son Ltd)

Hold your charcoal block together by purchasing or making a tray for it to sit in. (H.S. Walsh and Son Ltd)

the surface, but they are relatively expensive and tend to burn away if heat is applied for too long or they are left smouldering after use. To help the charcoal block last longer, keep a spray bottle handy and spray the block with water to stop it smouldering after it has been used. Wrapping binding wire around the blocks or sitting it in a small metal sheet with bent up edges or set it in plaster will hold the block together as it becomes thin or breaks. All these blocks will create small particle dusts when shaping or cutting, so do make sure you work in a well-ventilated area, wear a mask and avoid breathing in any of the dust.

Honeycomb block. (H.S. Walsh and Son Ltd)

Items can also be bound to the honeycomb brick using binding wire.

Honeycomb blocks can also be used but these are a little more expensive than standard heat reflective blocks and should be sitting on another surface when used, such as another heat reflective sheet or block. They are useful as they reflect the heat extremely well due to the holes in them, plus the holes can be used for pegs or binding the work directly to the block.

Heat reflecting from the surface you choose to heat on is important as it helps the soldering process progress a little quicker and helps the heat to spread evenly across the piece. After a bit of practice, experiment by sitting work on other materials. Some jewellers use pumice chunks, cat litter or ceramic chips. These are good at reflecting the heat in the same way as a honeycomb block, but can also be piled up to support more unusual shapes rather than flat pieces. Before you use the cat litter or ceramics chips, heat them up to ensure any moisture is removed, or it may pop and move the work when it is least expected.

Solder

When the work is ready to be soldered, before applying heat, the last element of setting up is to put the solder in place. Solder is usually placed where it can cross over the joint as it will flow between the contacting surfaces aided by the heat. Molten solder will flow towards the heat and when the flame is removed the solder solidifies. The solder will diffuse with the metal as the metal expands with the heat, then contracts again as it cools.

Solder can be bought in a variety of forms to enable different metals or combination of metals to be soldered. Silver solder is commonly used for silver, brass, copper and gilding metal. The step by step projects in this book will focus on silver solder; other types of soldering are introduced in Chapter Eight.

Silver solder can be purchased at a variety of melting temperatures and the higher the melting temperature the higher percentage of silver is contained in the solder. Sterling silver contains 7.5 per cent or less of copper. Mixing copper into the silver makes the metal stronger and allows the production of more delicate jewellery but also lowers the chance of the silver absorbing oxygen. Oxygen in the metal can make it porous and increases the risk of erosion. However, combining copper with the silver creates a further problem as copper oxide is formed when it is exposed to high temperatures, and even 1 per cent of copper oxide will make all the mix hard and brittle, even fragile. Copper oxide can also create fire scale on the metal. This removes the high reflectiveness of the silver, so be careful not to overheat your work when soldering. When making solder, the percentage of silver can remain the same, for example 65 per cent, and the other 35 per cent is made up of zinc and copper, with hard solder starting at about 29 per cent copper. To create solder, the zinc is added to the copper and silver alloy, with the zinc evaporating at low temperatures and absorbing into silver and copper. More zinc will create a lower melting temperature solder.

Enamelling solder has the highest melting temperature to ensure the work stays attached and is safe in the kiln while the glass enamels are fusing and melting into place. Enamels are usu-

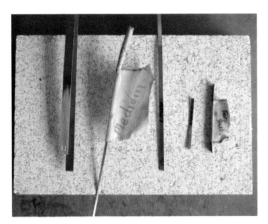

Silver solder.

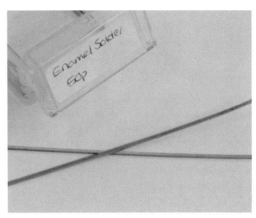

Enamel solder.

ally fired up to 800°C, so it is essential the joints and the metal do not move or distort during this process. To make the process easier when enamelling, try to use 97 per cent silver or fine silver for the metal and an enamel solder. Enamel solder melts when silver is at its cherry red state, so remove the flame as soon as you see the solder flow and be careful not to melt your work.

The next four solders are used for the majority of jewellery and silverwork and are a good place to start when learning. The four types are used in a decreasing order of hardness during the process of making a piece of work. In the UK, solder is given names for the different melting temperatures and is available at most jewellery and silver suppliers. In other countries the solder is sold by temperature or even made by the jeweller. Most jewellers buy solder in strips as this is the most economical way of purchasing silver solder and it is used for a huge variety of applications. However, it can also be bought as panels and wires, as well as a paste or in syringe. The paste and syringes are useful for particular applications such as soldering small items together or small items to large items. There are more details in Chapters Five and Six.

Sometimes it is difficult to remember which solder is which when you come to use it. When buying solder in strips in the UK, hard solder is the widest, medium the thinnest. However, it is still

recommended to label the solder as soon as possible. Find a method that suits your needs, either by stamping a letter into the solder itself, attaching a label or labelling the container you keep it in.

Hard solder has the highest melting temperature after enamel solder at around 770°C. It contains about 76 per cent silver mixed with

Stamping the letter H in the hard solder strip.

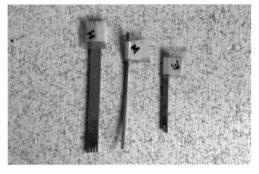

Tabs added to label silver solder strips.

Easy-flo solder.

other alloys. This means it will create the best colour match if you are soldering silver sheet, wire and tube and will be stronger than the other solder joints. Always start with hard solder, even if there is only one joint. If you have many solder joints, it is better to try to solder as many as possible with this solder, as each time it melts it diffuses deeper into the surface of the metal, making the melting temperature a little higher each time. This means fresh solder should melt before a joint that has already been made with hard solder. When soldering, sterling silver is heated to a temperature where the structure is open, allowing the solder to be drawn into the surface, mixing the solder and the silver together. Each time the joint is reheated the deeper the mix will go into the metal. A good joint should remain difficult to see when melted a few times. However, if you can see your solder line, the more you heat it the more porous the solder will become, revealing small dips in the surface of the joint.

Medium solder melts at around 750°C and contains about 70 per cent silver. It will be the thinnest strip when purchased and is usually used after hard solder to ensure the joints before do not become unattached or move. The lower percentage of silver in the solder, the more yellow the appearance, but with a really good close joint it should be almost invisible to the naked eye.

Easy solder has a melting temperature of around 710°C and has 60 per cent silver content. It will be more yellow than the higher melting temperature solders and will flow and join the metal before other joints melt, become unattached or move.

The last of the four is extra easy solder with the lowest melting temperature and silver content. It is recommended that it is only used for fixing jewellery. You will then be confident that it will not have been used in your own work and the joints will not dismantle when fixing work. Try not to use too much extra easy solder as this will also lower the percentage of silver in your work, which can affect the hallmark if it brings the overall percentage of silver in the piece below 92.5 per cent silver content.

There is one more silver solder, called 'easy flo'. This is usually used to solder silver to other metals, such as silver to steel. It works in a similar way to soft soldering and as it contains less than 50 per cent of silver, it is advisable to avoid using it on precious metal items, especially if you wish to hallmark them.

When setting up, most solder is applied in pallions or paillons. These are small rectangles of solder usually placed so they straddle the seam. A small amount of silver solder will flow a long way; some jewellers hammer or roll the solder to ensure they do not apply too much at once, whilst others cut the pallions or paillons straight from the bought strip so they are sure of the thickness they are using. In both cases, the solder needs to be clean before it is cut into small chips and fluxed in the same way the metal has been, ensuring it will flow and have the desired effect when heated. Try not to cut more solder off the strip than you need so the remaining solder does not go astray or get too dirty to use.

Place the solder with a pair of clean sharp tweezers or brush that is a little damp with flux, twisting the brush to remove the solder from the end or a solder pick that has a little flux on the tip to enable the solder to stick to it. Each of the

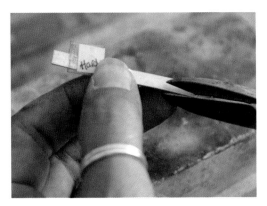

First cut the solder lengthways.

Cut multiple thin strips.

Then cut across the solder strip making a small collection of pallions/paillons.

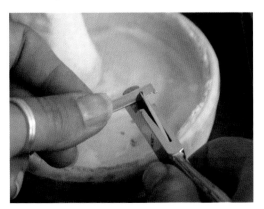

Using solder snips.

following step by step chapters will explain different ways of using the solder to join the metal and how to apply it. Before placing solder on your work, you may wish to consult the appropriate chapter for more details.

Making Tools

In all areas of jewellery, many tools are made for particular jobs or bought tools are adapted and changed to suit the maker's requirements and own ways of working. Tools made for soldering are easy to produce and can save lots of time. Some are to prevent the items moving when setting up or soldering and in turn

will avoid problems such as flooding of gaps, joints soldered at angles and out of place and smaller items clumping together never to be apart again. Spend a little time making a few tools to get started otherwise being caught without the right tools may mean using the first thing to hand. It will be a shame to heat a pair of favourite pliers, tempering the ends and softening them.

The soldering bricks and charcoal blocks can be adapted by cutting to shape with a jeweller's piercing saw, filed and drilled into, in order to hold, prop up and support work, and even old broken blocks are useful for various jobs. Broken saw blades are also useful for lifting work off the surface of the block or stopping tube or beads rolling around.

Home-made tools for holding work while soldering.

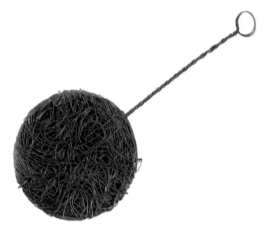

Soldering wigs can be made from binding wire or purchased already made. (H.S. Walsh and Son Ltd)

The soldering wig helps retain heat when soldering. (H.S. Walsh and Son Ltd)

Again, binding wire is useful, as well as holding work together or holding work to honeycomb bricks, it can be used to make something known as a soldering wig or soldering nest. A soldering wig is made up of loosely bound thin binding wire made into any shape that is about 4mm thick, enough to hold the work off the brick and allow the heat to be reflected from the brick on to the work. The soldering wig keeps hold of heat in a similar way to a charcoal block, after the heat is removed. This allows the flame to be moved around larger items without losing heat in one area. Unlike a charcoal block, a well-made soldering wig can last for years.

Cat litter is great for supporting work while soldering or even dampening a little to shape and hold a variety of items in place. Be sure to dry it out before applying direct heat to prevent any movement or popping. Cat litter works because it is basically a clay. The advantage of buying cat litter over clay is that it is very cheap and it is very easy to get hold of in small quantities. Plaster of Paris or casting plaster is also suitable and will be discussed later in the soldering small items section, Chapter Five. The plaster may take longer to dry, but gives a very secure hold on pieces of metal.

Other than the materials to support and hold work, jigs are useful to press lightly on work, clamp it and support it. Steel is an ideal material to use to make tools for a variety of reasons from cost, strength, weight, availability, lack of distortion when heat is applied, to the fact it will not draw heat out of the work and will not draw heat along it allowing it to be moved and changed at the cool end. Titanium is also extremely good, but a little harder to get hold of and shape. Look out for piano wire, steel straps, old clock springs, nuts, bolts, washers, old umbrella parts, bike parts, welding rod and cotter or split pins. All these can be adapted to make the ideal tool.

Strip of steel.

Steel strip bent in half.

Bent so ends meet at the tips.

Ends shaped and filed.

Here are a few tools you may wish to make yourself:

Tweezers

Tweezers can be made and adapted to hold a variety of shapes, wires and sheet together. The example described is ideal for holding sheet together or at 90 degrees to another surface.

1   Cut a strip of steel as wide as you would like your tweezers to be and slightly more than twice as long. Then bend the strip in half.

2   Bend the steel strip inwards about a third distance from the open end so the tips of the strip meet.

3   Cut, file and shape the ends of the strip for the job you have in mind.

4   A variety of these can be made with different tips and at different lengths to be used for different tasks.

Soldering Weight

The easiest way to hold work together is to rest one piece on top of another. A weight is useful too as it applies extra pressure to keep the items in place. This next tool is great for weighing something down and has minimum contact with the work. It can also be adapted extremely easily and quickly if problems occur. For example, use it to hold two or more pieces of sheet on to the soldering block, so they do not move while sweat soldering.

1   Cut a strip of steel roughly 15cm long and 1cm to 1.5cm wide.

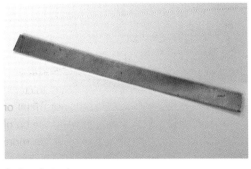

Strip of steel.

Cut and file a taper in the end.

Bend the steel 90 degree angles.

Put the tool in position to hold down items on the soldering brick.

2 Cut and shape one end into a taper with a rounded point so it will not scratch the object it will lean on, but has minimum contact with the surface.

3 Bend the tapered end 90 degrees at approximately a third of the length of the metal along from the point. Bend the wider end in the opposite direction also to 90 degrees to create a ledge on which to stack strips of metal or soldering bricks. It is useful to bend the tip of the strip up to hold the stack of blocks more securely on the end of the tool.

4 The blocks can either be made from the same strip that has been used to make the tool or a variety of thicknesses can be made to create different weights. Cut them a similar width as the tool for stability.

Cotter or split pin clamps

Cotter or split pin clamps are ideal for holding layers of sheet together. These can made to the size of the work and be adjusted to clamp reasonably tightly. Cotter pins are also useful to prop work on to lift it off the surface of a brick and enable the work to be heated from below.

1 Slot a nut on to a cotter pin; the nut should be able to slide along the cotter pin easily.

2 Bend the cotter pin 'legs' open, pushing the nut to the looped end of the pin.

A selection of copper/split pins and nuts.

Cotter pins with nuts slotted on.

Ends of the cotter pins pulled open.

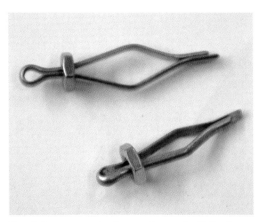

Bend the cotter pin tips so the ends sit flush together.

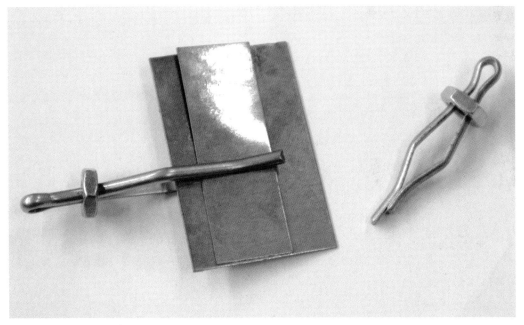

Clamping sheet together.

3 Bend the cotter pin 'legs' halfway along so the ends come back together at the tips.

4 Bend the cotter pin tips so the ends sit parallel and flush together.

5 Use the tool to clamp layers together. Push the nut along the length if a more secure grip is needed. These are particularly useful if more than one clamp is required.

Soldering pick. (H.S. Walsh and Son Ltd)

Soldering Pick

A soldering pick is a useful tool for moving a dislodged piece of solder, placing pressure on parts of the work while soldering and picking up and placing solder during the soldering process. It can also be used to aid solder to flow along a seam or in a cavity.

1   Cut a length of steel or titanium rod about a third longer than the tool you wish to finish with.

2   File the end of the steel or titanium rod to a point.

3   Bend the opposite end of the rod.

4   Create a handle or attach something to make the tool easy to hold.

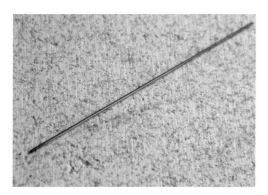

Length of steel rod.

Tapered end of steel rod.

Bend the end to make it easier to hold.

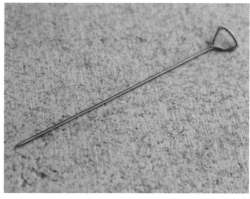

Finished soldering pick.

Reverse tweezers with stand.
(H.S. Walsh and Son Ltd)

Customized tweezers to hold two bits of round wire together.

Customizing Tweezers

Jewellers gather tools over years, either making their own for specific projects or adapting worn or cheap tools to their needs. Tweezers are ideal to adapt and adjust and can be purchased cheaply if you prefer not to make them from scratch.

Adding a stand to hold work in place or out of the way while soldering is extremely useful, especially if it can be adjusted or used in a variety of ways to provide different heights and angles.

Small pieces of wire are sometimes hard to hold together, especially with two flat edges of standard tweezers. To make it easier, tweezers can be bent and a semicircle can be filed into the tips to hold round wire securely.

If the round wire needs to be held at different angles the tweezer's ends can be bent and adjusted accordingly. Bending and filing tweezers in this way can save lots of time preparing and setting up your work and will add a nice array of tools to your tool box.

Other tools to help while soldering include items such as bench mates and third arms. You may wish to try borrowing a friend's or use other methods before spending the money on these items as they are not ideal for everyone and home-made tools can work just as well.

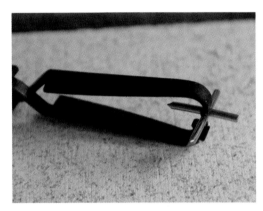

Customized tweezers holding wire at right angles.

Third hands are useful for holding tweezers at appropriate angles.

BASIC EDGE TO EDGE JOINT

The next few chapters will not only include information and tips, but also step by step projects involving some of the basic soldering processes. Plan all your designs from beginning to end on paper first, drawing your idea roughly and considering each step. When planning think of ways to avoid soldering and ways to add strength to joints with slots, folds and scored lines. Do not make work out of ten bits of metal when one piece does the same job. Consider elements that can be purchased, such as tubing. A variety of thicknesses and diameters can be purchased, and depending on the quantity required it can save a lot of work and is worth the extra expense if your design involves many tubular parts.

The soldering of edges is the most common solder joint. It is essential to ensure the pattern flows and the joint is invisible. If possible it is best to use one piece of metal rather than have a joint in it, but when making rings, tubes or rub over settings, attaching different metals together or joining scored edges, this is a necessary skill to practise. When making rings and stone settings it is important that you can make them to the right size and with an invisible joint.

Joining Pieces of Flat Metal

The first example will explain the general principles of soldering. The edge to edge joint is the weakest of all joints and it is worth considering how you would make this stronger for some applications. For example, a 'scarf joint' is when the metal is cut at an angle, allowing a larger surface of the metal to be joined, and a 'step joint' is when the ends are cut with two levels,

OPPOSITE PAGE: **Basic edge to edge joint.**

RIGHT: **Joining pieces of flat metal.**

overlapping the edges. These are sometimes only possible with thicker sheets of metal and with practice, as precise work is required. Other options could be considered to strengthen the joint that affect the aesthetics and it is worth considering how the added details will add to the overall design. For example, the edges can completely overlap each other or an extra piece added overlapping both ends; this is often called a 'strap joint'.

1 Ensure the edges that are going to be joined fit together, file them if not. Even a small gap can cause problems when soldering or result in an unsightly flaw. If you have filed them then this will also clean any grease and dirt away.

2 If the edges are flat you may still need to clean them as described in Chapter 2. For this example, wet or dry paper on a flat surface has been used to keep the edges sharp and fitting together well.

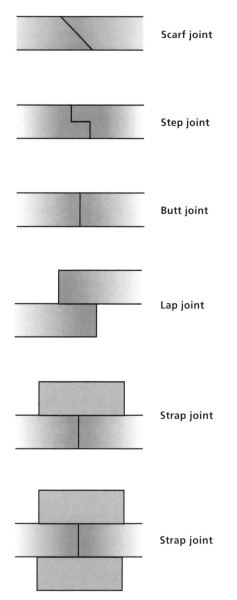

Scarf joint

Step joint

Butt joint

Lap joint

Strap joint

Strap joint

A variety of joints.

File the edges to make sure they are flat.

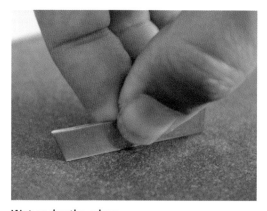

Wet or dry the edges.

Wash your hands to ensure that the flux or work does not get any grease or dirt on them.

If needed pin the work to the heat reflective brick.

3   Wash your hands to ensure you do not contaminate the flux or work with any grease or dirt for the next stage of the process.

4   Put the work on the chosen heat reflective surface. Here we are starting simply with a standard heat reflective soldering brick. Pin the pieces if they need to be held in place. This will depend on size, the heavier the pieces the less likely they are to move.

5   Apply flux to the edges of the metal where it is going to be soldered. For this example borax is used. Borax may bubble and move when first heated, but it will also take a while to burn away, making it a good flux to practise with.

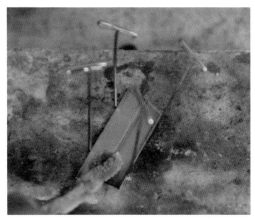

Flux the joint.

6   Place a small piece of solder overlapping the joint; take some time to think about this. Consider where would be the easiest place to clean up the solder if it flowed a little in the wrong direction. For this example, the solder is placed at one end of the joint, as it is easier to clean the end of the finished item rather than the middle. Hard solder is used as this is the only joint that is going to be made on this piece.

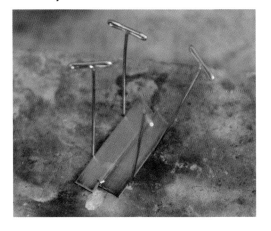

Place the solder so it will be easier to clean up later.

Heat the work with a bushy flame, if your torch is not adjustable start with it a little further away.

Remove the heat when the solder has flowed.

Let the work cool before moving it.

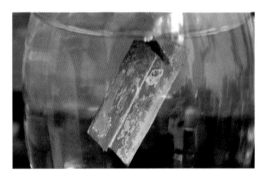

Then cool completely in water.

7 Heat the metal with a bushy flame; this is known as a reducing flame, which means it is using a lot of fuel and in turn absorbs the oxides that stop the solder flowing. The bushy flame will allow both pieces of metal to be heated at the same time to the same temperature. There is no advantage of heating it up fast with a hotter flame. Apply the heat to the whole piece, moving the flame constantly across the work as if painting the metal with the flame. Use the midpoint of the flame rather than the tip or right up to the torch end and move away a little if the metal is heating up too fast. Remember to heat the metal not the solder; the metal should be able to transfer the heat to the solder. If both pieces are the same temperature the solder will flow along the joint. Remove the flame when the solder has flowed. If you have a longer join, heat the metal slightly more where you want the solder to flow as it will flow towards the heat.

8 When the redness of the metal has dulled, cool the work in water. It is advisable not to put hot metal straight into the pickle, as mentioned in Chapter One.

9 Place your piece in a warmed pickle solution. Remember to use brass, copper, wooden or plastic tweezers as steel may create a reaction

Place the piece in warmed pickle solution.

in the solution and plate the pieces with a layer of copper.

10 Remove the metal from the pickle when all the oxides and flux residue have gone. Copper will look a little pink while silver will look white at this stage.

11 Rinse your work thoroughly. You may want to also scrub it a little with a nylon brush, water and pumice to ensure all the dirt and pickle has been removed.

Remove from pickle when oxides and flux residue have gone.

USE A BUSHY FLAME

Remember the equipment section of this book, which stated 'the lower flow temperature of the pewter solder will create a weaker bond more like glue' when using it to solder other metals. A pointy hot flame heats silver solder too fast, creating a similar bond. It causes the solder to flow, but not permeate the surface of both pieces of metal. This may be strong with a little wiggle test but later one piece may break cleanly away from the other.

Rinse to remove any traces of pickle.

Joining the Two Ends of a Ring

Rings are measured and shaped in a variety of ways and, just like most processes in jewellery making, there are always alternative methods. Practice will help discover the method that works best for you. The first few stages of this step by step solder joining process is to show how the joint can be cut with no gaps first time.

1 Bend the metal to size so the edges are overlapping a small amount. Practise with overlapping only a few millimetres to prevent wasting metal, especially if you are working with precious metals.

A plain copper ring.

Overlap the ends of the strip before cutting.

Cut through both layers of the overlapping joint.

2 Cut the metal through both layers. The metal will be cut at the same angle in all directions and allows for slight wobbles or cutting angles to still fit tightly together. If the metal has been cut before shaping and bending it, you will need to ensure the edges meet perfectly. A simple way of doing this is to cut back into the joint with the saw blade. It may require a few attempts, but is much easier than unbending, filing and bending back in the hope that the edges fit well.

3 Bend the edges so they align perfectly with no gaps or overhang. Depending on the thickness of the metal being used this can be done without tools and just using your fingers or using ring pliers. If using ring pliers keep the curved edge on the inside of the ring so the metal does not get marked or dented.

4 As the edges have just been cut they are already clean and free from grease. Wash your hands to ensure you do not contaminate the flux or work with any grease or dirt for the next stage of the process. Then apply flux to the joint. The flux will get drawn into the joint in the same way the solder will when heating so there is no need to open the ring flux and bend back.

Use ring pliers to align the ends of the ring.

Flux the edges of the metal to be joined.

Sit a piece of solder on the heat reflective brick.

Sit the joint on top of the solder.

5   Place a piece of solder on a heat reflective brick. Try to estimate the quantity that will be required to join the two edges together. You can always add more solder if there is not enough. Remember, it will take more work to remove any excess solder.

6   Place the ring on its edge with the joint sitting directly on to the piece of solder. It is easier to balance the ring on the solder rather than the solder on the ring. For large thin metal rings or boxes, binding wire may be required to hold the joint together while being heated. Standard rings are made with a 1.2mm or thicker sheet or wire; this should hold its shape while being soldered without any need to clamp or hold it.

Warm the whole piece.

7   Heat the metal with a bushy flame. Apply the heat to the whole piece, moving the flame constantly around the ring as if painting the metal with the flame. When the metal starts to glow dark red move the flame across the two ends of the ring, moving back and forth.

8   Watch the solder carefully. When the ring is hot enough the solder will melt and run very fast up the joint. Remove the heat as soon as this happens.

Watch as the solder runs up the joint.

Let the redness of the metal dull.

Quench the piece in the water.

Then place it in warm pickle.

Remove from the pickle and rinse thoroughly.

9 Let the redness of the metal dull before moving the work. This will allow the solder to solidify and the metal will cool evenly.

10 Finish cooling the metal in water. As mentioned previously, do not to put hot metal straight into the pickle.

11 Once cooled place your piece in a warmed pickle solution to remove any flux and oxides.

12 When the copper has turned pink or the silver turned white, remove the work from the pickle and rinse well in water.

13 There are many options for finishing, the main area that will need attention is the joint. For flat surfaces it is easier to apply wet or dry paper to a stick to create an even surface with which to sand the metal. To attach the paper, double sided tape or glue is recommended to make sure there are no lumps or overlaps on the stick. The joint of the ring will completely disappear if you have soldered silver, or an extremely thin silver line will be visible if soldering other metals with silver solder.

Use wet or dry paper to even the surfaces by the joint.

14 For the inside of the ring, wet or dry paper stuck to a half round or round stick can be used to keep the shape of the ring. If the ridge is a little deep start with either rougher paper or even a file and work through each paper grade down to the finest paper before polishing.

15 If you are going to wear copper, brass or gilding metal then do be aware that it can make your skin green where your skin and the metal touch.

Use a round stick to sand the inside of the ring.

TOO MUCH HEAT

Continuing to heat the metal after the solder has flowed can cause two problems. One can be disastrous and cause the piece to melt. The other problem can occur when using silver, creating something called fire stain. Fire stain is when the copper in the silver causes a grey pinkish surface. This can be cleaned and polished away, but cleaning and polishing it will start to remove any textures or patterns already applied to the surface.

Ring being worn after sanding with fine wet or dry paper.

Soldering a Rub Over Setting or Edge in Place

Strips made into stone settings or shapes are a great way to create a feature on a piece of jewellery. The space left can be filled with a stone or various materials such as resins, or left as a decoration.

1 Make the setting and attach the ends in the same way as soldering the ends of a ring. It may be easier to shape when the ends have been soldered.

2 Make sure the edges of the setting are flat and clean. It is easier to do this by putting the paper on to a flat surface and rubbing the pieces on it.

Soldering edges for stones or to hold resins.

Make and solder the shapes in the same way as soldering two ends of a ring.

Clean the edges to be soldered on to the flat surface.

Clean the flat surfaces where the shapes will be soldered.

Dip the shapes into the flux.

Place the solder on the joint, choose the inside or the outside of the shape carefully.

3   Clean the surface of the flat piece to which the setting is to be soldered.

4   Flux the pieces on the edges and on the flat surface. It is easier to do this by dipping the setting into the flux.

5 Place the solder on the joint on the inside or the outside of the setting. Choose a place where the metal will be covered up or removed, or where it is easier to clean.

6 Warm the flux to make sure it holds the solder in place.

7 Heat the setting and the metal base to the same temperature until the solder flows. You may want to lift the piece to heat it from underneath or set it up raised from the soldering brick before you start.

Tubes and scored edges are soldered using these processes, too. Tube can also be purchased in a variety of thicknesses and diameters. As mentioned previously, it is worth planning all your designs from beginning to end, drawing your idea out and consider each step before you begin. Avoid soldering and add strength if possible. Wearable pieces are bashed and knocked more than the wearer may notice. Extra strength will save unhappy friends and customers and avoid you needing to spend time fixing.

Warm the flux to hold the solder in place.

To heat the piece underneath you may want to lift the work or place in on a split pin.

SWEAT SOLDERING

Sweat soldering is the name given to the process of melting solder on to a flat surface, then reheating it to join it to another flat surface. The advantage of sweat soldering rather than basic soldering is it avoids the spread of the solder across the exposed surfaces.

Sweat soldering also allows metal sheets to be stacked. Makers who are particularly practised at this, develop their skills to produce metal sheets that have a patterned surface similar to a decorative wood grain. This process originated from Japan and is called mokume gane. Different coloured metals are stacked and usually fused or soldered, then hammered, twisted and rolled to create wonderful patterned metals.

If stacked metals are to be soldered, the surface of each piece of metal except the first is completely flooded with hard or medium solder, then pickled, rinsed well and fluxed. The layers are then stacked together and bound tightly with heavy gage steel wire and heated until each layer is soldered to the next. An alternative method is to clean each layer and flux well. Solder is then rolled out into a thin sheet to the same dimensions as the layers; it is also cleaned and flux is placed between each layer. Again, it is bound with steel wire and heated until all the layers are soldered. Small quantities of mokume gane can be purchased from very specialist suppliers. If using bought or home-made mokume gane in your work, paint an inhibitor or white

out over the areas not being soldered to ensure the layers do not lift apart.

Inhibitors are very useful when protecting previously soldered joints, keeping areas with textures from being flooded with solder, links and hinges from joining together or thin areas from becoming overheated. Some inhibitors are also used to protect gemstones and alternative materials from becoming hot and cracking or heat coloured. However, use all inhibitors with caution; if you are heating your metal to enable you to solder, you are likely to be heating the whole piece and the metal can transfer the heat easily to everything it touches.

Stopping solder from travelling where it is not wanted is one of the most common reasons to use an inhibitor. Cigarette papers used to be put between hinge joints to stop the solder flowing and joining the knuckles to the wrong part of lockets and boxes, however safer options are now available. Rouge powder mixed with water and a drop of methylated spirits became the next

Sweat soldered.

OPPOSITE PAGE: **Sterling silver and mokume gane cuff by Leigh Nicole Leal.**

Thermo gel. (H.S. Walsh and Son Ltd)

popular mixture, as they were both substances in most jewellers' workshops. However, white out or correction fluid works just as well by making the surface dirty so solder will not flow on to it and it protects already soldered joints and components. It has the added advantage as it can be easily painted on to surfaces with accuracy. There are also inhibitors that can be bought at most jewellery suppliers. Thermo Gel can be used for all the purposes mention

above. A centimetre-thick layer of gel is applied to stones and joints to protect them during soldering; afterwards the gel washes away easily with water.

Joining a Small Flat Piece to a Large Flat Piece

1   To practise sweat soldering, start with one layer, as this is a great process to give your pieces depth. Different metals, layers with different textures, pierced layers and layers with varying thicknesses are worth considering to help enhance your designs.

2   Ensure the flat surfaces that are going to be joined are completely flat. The easiest way to sand the surfaces is to lay wet or dry paper on a flat surface such as glass, metal or wood, then rub the metal on the paper. Doing this will also ensure the metal is clean. A 400 grit paper provides a good surface for the solder to flow compared with a highly polished surface. However, try not to ruin the surface that you wish to be visible after everything has been joined. When the surfaces are satisfactory, wash your hands to ensure you do not contaminate the flux or work with any grease or dirt for the next stage of the process.

3   Apply flux to the surfaces of the metal where it is going to be soldered. For this example borax is used. Borax may bubble and move when first heated, but it will also take a while to burn away, making it a good flux to practise with.

4   Put the small piece of metal on the chosen heating surface.

5   Place enough solder on the metal sheet to ensure when it melts it will cover all the

Sweat soldering.

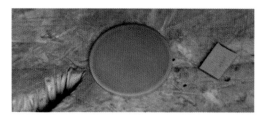

Two cleaned flat surfaces.

Apply flux to the areas to be joined.

Small piece on heat reflective brick.

Place solder on the small metal sheet.

Heat until the solder has run over the surface of the metal.

surface. If there are parts of the shape that extrude from the main part of the sheet make sure there are pallions on them, too.

6   Heat the metal with a bushy flame; remember you are heating the metal not the solder and the solder will melt on to the sheet. Heat it until the solder has spread nicely across the surface. If you are using large items and find the solder does not spread, you may wish to file the surface with a criss-cross pattern to encourage the solder to flow across the surface or use the solder pick to encourage the solder to spread. Let the piece cool a little.

7   Apply a little more flux to the small piece and place it in position on the larger piece on the heating surface. You may need to raise the item off the surface a little to enable the large piece to heat up at the same speed as the top smaller piece. Here you may want to use a honeycomb block, soldering wig or just prop up the work with a split pin or wire, depending on the size.

8   Heat both pieces of metal; the smaller piece will heat up quicker, so ensure you move the flame around all the work to allow them to heat up evenly. The solder on the back of the small piece will melt on to the surface of the larger piece. Watch the work carefully as a very thin line of flowing silver solder will be just visible at the bottom of the small piece.

Place in position on to larger piece.

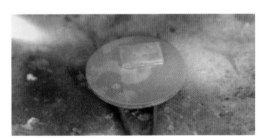

Heat from underneath until a small silver line appears at the bottom edge of the small piece.

STOPPING SOLDER FLOW

Substances can be applied to the surface of metal to stop the solder flowing, such as white out, rouge powder, pencil lead and graphite sticks and crayons. This is not needed for sweat soldering, but can be extremely useful when soldering highly textured surfaces to stop the solder filling the texture and to stop parts of hinges from soldering together or to the wrong side of the hinge and to stop pieces that are meant to have moving parts becoming joined. Some jewellers will also cover areas already soldered to stop previous solder flowing, too.

SOLDERING SMALL ITEMS

At some point you will need to solder small items and care needs to be taken to ensure the piece does not melt into a ball. There are various options to assist the ease of soldering small items and practice with all of them would help find a way that suits each project. The first option would be to consider leaving extra metal on pieces while soldering. This can be removed afterwards and there are added advantages to doing this, such as the excess part can be clamped, held or used to support the work.

Try not to be enticed into purchasing small items and findings such as jump rings, stone settings and earring wires. It is worth spending a little time considering what shape, form and thickness will enhance your design and create something unique for the wearer.

If you have a deep pickle bath you may also require an additional tool when making small items. A pickle basket, sieve or tea strainer is very useful for keeping the small items together and to make it easier to lift them in and out of the pickle solution. Alternatively, items such as jump rings can be slotted on to a piece of wire that then has the two ends twisted together.

Soldering Jump Rings

There are a variety of ways to making and soldering jump rings. To keep it simple and focus on the soldering process we will stick to circular in shape and use round wire, shaped using round nose pliers and cut with a piercing saw along the length of the spiral.

Cutting jump rings.

1 Take a piece of copper wire and clean one end. This can be the same thickness or a little thinner than the jump rings you have made.

Clean piece of copper wire.

OPPOSITE PAGE: **Feather Series, by Christine Johnson.**

2 Flux the clean one end of the copper wire and clamp the other end in a pair of tweezers.

Hold the wire in a pair of tweezers.

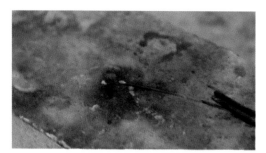

Melt solder on to the end of the wire.

Hold the jump rings in a pair of reversible tweezers.

Apply flux to the jump rings.

3 Hold the wire on to a piece of solder and heat it gently to attach the solder to the copper wire. Put this to one side while you prepare the jump rings.

4 If you have just made your jump rings, the ends to be soldered will be clean. Wash your hands to ensure you do not contaminate the flux or work with any grease or dirt for the next stage of the process. Hold the jump rings in a pair of reversible tweezers or a split pin. The tweezers need to clamp the jump rings at the opposite side to the joint.

5 Apply flux to the jump rings. It will be drawn into the joints.

6 Hold the copper wire with the solder on the end on the jump ring joint. Heat the wire and jump ring with a bushy flame; a little of the solder will transfer from the wire to the jump ring.

7 Move the wire as soon as solder has transferred and move on to the next jump ring.

8 Pickle and clean up the jump rings as required. If soldering a jump ring to another piece, consider soldering the joint and attaching it at the same time, as described in Chapter Six. If you are making a chain, solder half the jump rings as described above, then link two soldered rings on to an open ring to make groups of three. Then link two groups of three to an open ring and so on, until you have reached the desired length of chain.

Heat the ring while the copper wire is held on to the joint.

Move to the next joint as soon as a little of the solder has transferred, use this wire until all the solder has transferred.

Soldering a chain.

WORKING WITH SMALL PIECES OF METAL

Shape, form and solder small items while they are still attached to the original piece of metal. This can form a handle to help move and hold it easily, cutting the excess off at the last possible moment.

Soldered jump rings.

Soldering Lots of Small Parts Together

As well as soldering jump rings, you may need to solder one small item to another. The main problem arises when heat is applied and parts start to move because of the flux drying out, the torch blowing them about or the solder creating a pool to allow them to slide about. If you only have two or three elements you may find that the jigs and tools in Chapter Two will solve these problems, however when soldering a lot of small elements the following strategy may be easier.

1   Clean all the small parts to be joined together and coat them in flux.

Soldering lots of small parts.

2   Warm the parts to ensure the flux is coating all the areas where they will be soldered.

Clean and flux all the wires.

6 Fill the well with plaster of Paris or casting plaster and allow it to set. In the USA there is also a soldering investment available from some suppliers that can be used instead. Ensure the plaster is entirely dry. You may need to remove the modelling clay or wax when it has set and leave a little longer to allow all the water to evaporate. Try to keep the thickness of plaster to 2cm or less to reduce the drying time.

Warm the flux so it adheres to the wire

Press wire into the modelling clay.

3 Roll out some modelling clay or soft wax; ensure it is even and flat.

4 Press the metal parts halfway into the surface in the desired design layout. Lay them out with all the parts touching at least one other part and facing up as if you were looking at the front of the finished piece.

5 Build a small modelling clay, card or wax wall around the edge of the work to create a well.

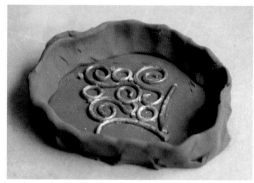

Make a modelling clay wall around the piece.

Roll out some modelling clay.

Fill the well with plaster.

Remove the modelling clay and let the piece dry.

Heat the work until all the joints are soldered.

Place solder on every joint.

9 Plunge the entire piece into water to quench, allowing the plaster to break away from the metal. Put the broken plaster in the bin rather than leave it in the sink as it can sit in pipes and clog them.

10 Clean the piece up carefully. It may be easier to put the piece on a flat surface to ensure the work does not get bent or distorted.

Warm the plaster and the work to ensure all the moisture has been removed.

Plunge the entire piece into water to break away the plaster.

7 Clean all traces of wax and modelling clay away from the joints with a fine blade and remove any traces of grease. Flux each joint and place a small piece of solder where required.

8 Warm the work with a bushy flame first to ensure all moisture has been removed from the plaster. Heating it too quickly may cause the plaster to crack as the water tries to escape. Heat the entire work until all joints are soldered.

Clean the piece carefully, you will need to remove the remains of the plaster.

ATTACHING FIXINGS AND FINDINGS

In a similar way to the previous chapter there is a danger of melting small items into a ball. This is even easier when trying to solder small items to large items as you try to heat the large item to the temperature required.

Many mass produced findings will be silver-plated. If you try to solder these to your work, the thin layer of plating is likely to burn away, exposing the base metal underneath. The joint may then be weak as the solder melts to the plated layer or the burnt residue rather than the base metal. There are also mass produced earring posts and cufflink backs that have a disc of silver attached. Avoid these too as they are usually soldered with easy or extra easy solder and can easily come away while they are being soldered to the main body of the piece.

Swivel cufflink backs contain a small piece of steel that acts as a spring. If this is overheated it will soften and make the attachment loose. If you are attaching this type of back, try not to heat the torpedo section of the cufflink back or purchase a set that requires the torpedoes to be attached by riveting after everything has been soldered together. Or better yet, design and make an alternative fixture to complement your design.

Remember to plan your design carefully before you start and consider if the fixtures and findings work well with the overall look. You may want your fixtures and findings to enhance the design and meaning or to disappear and be almost invisible. You will also need to consider the body and how work attaches and hangs when it is worn, for example place horizontal brooch backs and earring posts above the centre line of the entire piece to ensure the top does not tilt forward when wearing it. Also, for horizontal brooch backs place the catch on the left-hand side and the hinge on the right when looking at the back of the brooch to make sure it is easy for a right-handed person to attach to their clothes.

Soldering Earring Posts on to an Earring

Attaching an earring post is an example of when you are likely to need to solder a small item on to a larger item. Earring posts are usually made from 0.7mm or 0.8mm thick wire, with a small ridge a few millimetres in from the outer end

Attaching an earring post.

OPPOSITE PAGE: **Attaching fixings and findings.**

Clean the metal and the post.

Hold the post in a pair of reverse action tweezers.

Apply flux on the post and on the piece where you would like it to be soldered.

to help hold the scroll or earring back in place. Avoid purchasing ready-made earring posts and get into the habit of making your own as you need them; they can then be designed and made to fit in with your designs to the thickness required and they will also be a lot cheaper.

1 Ensure the metal is clean in the area you wish the post to be fixed and at the end of the post. Wash your hands to ensure you do not contaminate the flux or work with any grease or dirt for the next stage of the process.

2 Hold the earring post in a pair of reverse action tweezers. The tweezers need to clamp the post at the opposite end you wish to attach to the earring, at the end with the ridge.

3 Apply flux to the surface of the metal where the post is going to be soldered and on the end of the earring post.

For the next three stages there are a few options:

Option One

4 Sit the earring post on a small piece of solder and warm it enough to fuse the solder to the end of the post.

5 Sit the earring on a split pin and the post on the earring.

6 Heat the metal with a bushy flame, heating the earring not the post. The solder on the post will melt on to the sheet. Heating the work from below is called conduction soldering. This is also good for delicate work such as filigree.

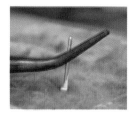

First attach the solder to the post.

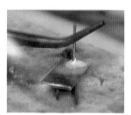

Heat the piece from underneath by sitting it on a split pin.

Remove the heat as soon as the solder has flowed.

Melt the solder on to the post.   **Heat the earring to a dull red.**

Hold the earring in place until the solder has flowed.

Option Two

4   Sit the earring post on a small piece of solder and warm it enough to fuse the solder to the end of the post.

5   Sit the earring on the soldering surface and practise holding the post in place. Then heat the surface until it is a dull red.

6   Bring the post into place and hold until the solder has flowed. Keep hold until the piece has cooled and the solder is no longer molten.

Option Three

4   Sit the earring on the soldering surface and place the solder where the post will be attached. Practise holding the post in place.

5   Heat the earring until the solder has balled and is ready to melt. Bring the post into place and wait a few seconds for the post to warm up and join to the earring.

6   Remove the heat as soon as the joint is connected.

 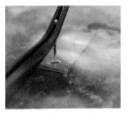

Put the solder in place on the earring.   **Heat until the solder has joined the post and the earring together.**

Keep the post in place until the redness has gone from the metal and the solder is no longer molten.

ANNEALING

This process is used by jewellers and metalsmiths to soften the metal in order to make it easier to shape and work with it. It also allows it to be worked without causing cracks or stress points. When an item is soldered, it also anneals the metal, putting it back into its low stress state, and this can cause problems if the aim is to use the metal as a catch, or to use the work-hardened metal to keep the shape and strength. There are a few options to avoid this happening or to rectify the problem. The solution will depend on the overall aim, but consider burnishing and barrel polishing items when finished, lightly hammering ear wires or finding alternative ways of joining.

STICK FEEDING

Stick feeding is the only silver soldering process in which the solder is not cut into small squares and instead is cut into a thin long strip and held into a joint as it is heated. This process is used to join two pieces that have no surface or edge to balance solder on when setting up. It is commonly used in silversmithing when soldering seams, spheres and curved surfaces.

You may also wish to use a turntable to sit your work on. Turntables make it easier to rotate the work while it is being heated, allowing the solder to flow around the entire circumference of the piece.

A steady hand and good heat control are essential when using the stick feeding process. Practise holding the solder in place before applying the heat and if possible use something to prop your hand on. Alternatively clamp the tweezers in a third hand at a right angle and at a height to enable it to be easily put in position and removed when necessary.

If you find your solder and hand warming up before any solder has melted into the join, try to move the hand holding the torch closer to the hand holding the solder. This will ensure the heat is pointing at the work and away from you and your hands.

1   Ensure the edges are flat and clean and sit together tightly. If the two or more pieces create a sealed hollow form, ensure that a hole

Soldered domes.

Small turntable with soldering block on top.

OPPOSITE PAGE: **Stick feeding.**

Wet or dry the edges of the dome and make sure they are flat.

Flux the edges to be soldered, sometimes this is easier by putting them into the flux dish.

Place items on to the solder brick.

or gap is made in one of the surfaces to allow air to escape. Air expands when it is heated and the form is likely to pop or explode to allow the air to escape if it is soldered completely closed.

2 Larger items may need to be bound together with binding wire, however smaller items can sit together on the soldering surface. Flux the edge and it will be drawn into the joint.

3 If possible use a small turntable underneath the soldering surface to enable the work to be rotated as the solder runs around the joint.

4 Clamp a thin strip of cleaned and fluxed solder in a pair of reverse action tweezers.

5 Heat the work slowly, rotating it to enable the metal to heat evenly.

6 When the two pieces reach a dull red colour, hold the solder on the joint, removing it as soon as a few millimetres have melted into the joint. Rotate the work, heating the area just in front of where the solder has flowed. Molten solder will flow towards heat; if the solder stops flowing and more needs to be added hold the solder back on the joint where required. Remember to feed the solder into an area where it will be easier to clean up if the solder spreads a little.

Clamp a thin strip of solder into the tweezers.

Heat the work slowly moving the flame around the top and bottom pieces.

When the work is red, place the solder into the joint and remove as soon as a small piece of solder has flowed.

SOLDERING LARGER ITEMS

Remember the preparation and set up for soldering is as important as heating the work. Careful planning will save a lot of time and avoid the likelihood of any mishaps.

When soldering larger items, you may wish to have some extra tools to hand around the soldering area in case you need them while you are heating up your work. Your hand-made weights and tools may be useful for example, to encourage solder to run; some are useful to hold work in place and others can be used as a heat sink to make sure the heat does not get lost through the other end of your piece.

You may also wish to use the stick feeding process to add more solder when you have not quite placed enough on the work while setting up. This is more common while soldering larger items and can be easily resolved by having a pair of tweezers with the solder strip clamped in it to hand to enable you to add a little more when required.

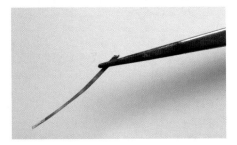

Clamp the solder strip in tweezers to allow you to add a little more when you need to.

OTHER METALS AND TECHNIQUES

This chapter will encourage you to try some more advanced techniques and get you started when wanting to experiment with other metals than the ones used in previous chapters of this basic book. It will also give a few solutions to problems you may be having with silver soldering. When you have had a go you may want to read about them in more depth to see how you can develop a better and deeper understanding.

Untitled, by Maya Antoun.

Advanced Techniques

This will cover processes that can be used in jewellery and require the use of solder, but do not fit in the standard jewellery soldering categories. They will also help encourage you to try different techniques by using solder and the soldering process.

Solder Inlays and Inlaying

Inlaying is a specialist process in which one material is inserted into a contrasting material. Solder inlays are fun and a nice way of highlighting patterns in copper and brass surfaces. Shapes and patterns are pressed or stamped into the surface and filled with silver solder.

Stamp or roll patterns into the metal.

OPPOSITE PAGE: **Pair of Crows by Rebecca Skeels.**

1   Stamp the desired patterns into the surface of the metal.

2   Ensure the inclines are clean and free from dirt and grease. It may be easier to use a fibreglass brush to get into all the smaller spaces. Ensure you wear gloves when working with a glass brush and work on a surface that can be easily cleaned or disposed of, as the small fibres from the brush can easily irritate skin and are not easy to see.

3   Flux in the dips where you wish it to be highlighted with silver and place a piece of solder in each one.

4   Heat the piece until the solder floods the inside of each dip. Do not worry if some overflow. If the solder does not run into all the edges, use a solder pick to encourage it.

5   File and sand the solder or surface of the metal back. Over time, the copper will darken and oxidize, making the silver solder inlay more prominent.

Flux the dips and place solder in each one.

Heat the piece evenly.

Fibreglass brush, (H.S. Walsh and Son Ltd)

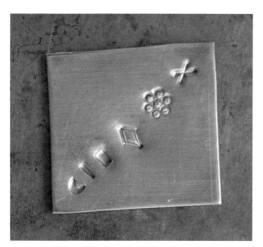

Ensure all the dips are clean.

Until all the solder has flowed.

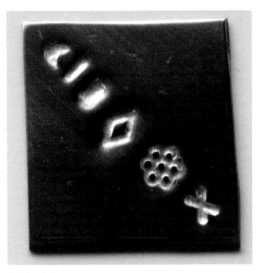

Solder inlay.

Sand back the surface of the solder and metal.

Filigree

Filigree is another very specialist process and is worth reading more about if you are interested in developing the technique further. It is a process using small thin wires, twisting and scrolling to create delicate lattice work. This is then either soldered on to another surface or into a framework. The process explained below is one way of soldering the delicate pieces together. Other techniques are used for this process: for example, some jewellers solder gold lattice work to copper and then etch the copper away, leaving the gold.

Simple filigree.

1 Solder the filigree framework using the previous step by step projects in this book and place the filigree in place.

2 File the solder over a piece of paper to create a solder dust. Use easy solder if possible as it is easier to use a solder that has a larger gap between solder melting temperature and material melting temperature.

Solder the framework using the previous step by step projects; the frame can be with or without a backing.

3 Paint the filigree with flux and then dust the surface of the filigree with the filings rather than using chips of solder as in previous projects.

4 Heat the whole piece carefully, moving the flame constantly over the whole piece of the work. Remember, the small wire elements will heat up quickly. If the work is on a metal backing it will help to heat the piece from underneath.

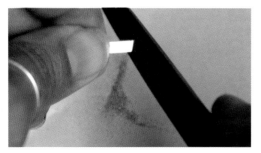

Make the solder into dust by filing it over a piece of paper.

Paint the filigree with flux and dust with solder.

Heat the whole piece until the solder has flowed.

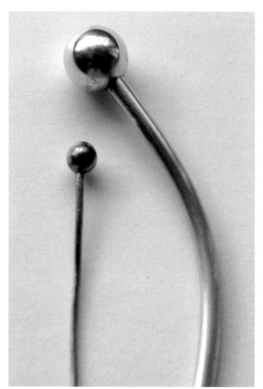

Soldering a bead on to a wire.

Soldering on a Bead or Ball

A traditional bangle design has balls or beads soldered to the open ends. Bangles are one of the jewellery items most susceptible to damage from wear and tear. To ensure the bead is soldered on without causing an enclosed hollow there is a simple and effective process. An enclosed hollow is likely to explode or pop when heated, as the air will try to escape as the air expands. To ensure this does not happen, a hole or gap needs to be planned to allow the air to escape.

1 Taper the end of the wire just enough for it to easily push through the hole in the bead and protrude from the other side.

2 Clean the end of the wire and the hole in the ball or bead. Then wash your hands.

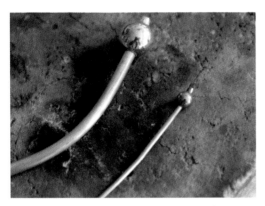

Taper the ends of the wire so they just fit through the holes in the bead

Clean the end of the wire and the holes in the beads.

3   Flux and solder the protruding end allowing the air to escape from the unsoldered end of the bead.

4   Heat the wire and the bead to the same temperature until the solder has flowed.

5   Cut off the excess wire and clean up the surface to the desired finish.

Fusing

Fusing is different from soldering as it does not use another metal to fill the joint. It is a localized process using a hot flame to heat two surfaces until they become fluid. This causes the two surfaces to diffuse together and create a joint as strong as the metal itself. However, the

Flux and place a piece of solder on the outer edge of the bead

Heat the wire and bead until the solder has flowed.

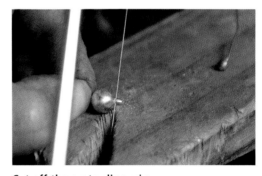

Cut off the protruding wire

File and sand the end to match the rest of the bead.

process of fusing creates a risk of the components being melted, as the temperature used to fuse is the same as the melting point of the metal being used.

Processes such as Keum-boo and granulation commonly use fusing to create specialist effects rather than soldering. Keum-boo results in silver or brass having a thin gold leaf layer applied to the surface. The two metals then unite, creating an even and flush joint. If solder was used, it would be likely to create an uneven surface as well as lift the gold away from the parent metal, creating a risk of burning the thin leaf as it is heated.

Granulation is where small beads or chips are attached to a piece to decorate it. Fusing has the advantage here so that the bead is only joined at the point of contact to the parent metal, while solder could fill some of the small gaps, changing the aesthetics and shape of the beads.

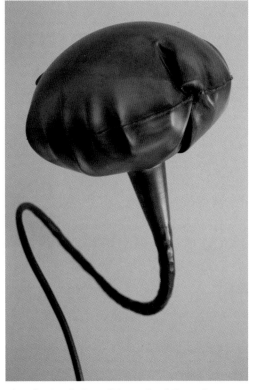

Blow by Mark Gray. (Photo: Paul Kenny)

Welding

Welding uses heat and/or pressure, with and without additional materials. For example, forge welding heats the metal until it becomes white with heat and then applies a pressure through hammering or pressing to get it to unite together. This is very similar to fusing, however many jewellery processes do not apply pressure when fusing.

Like fuse welding, this creates the risk of melting the work due to the high temperatures used. However, it is a popular process for metals such as steel. Steel is a poor conductor of heat and allows the areas that are being welded to be the only part of the piece to require heating when they are joined.

Welding can also be done with electricity. This is common when welding steel commercially or when using a spot welder. However, with the development of processes and technology, miniature arc welders such as the PUK and laser welders have been developed for the jewellery industry.

Precious metals such as platinum and palladium are welded either using an oxygen flame to achieve the high temperatures or a micro welder. The micro welder produces a very small hot flame and is often used to repair jewellery items, but can be used for small soldering jobs, too.

Micro welder at the School of Craft and Design at the University for the Creative Arts in Farnham.

Gluing

Gluing is extremely useful when attaching different materials together, for holding items in place temporarily and adding colour and highlights into dips and spaces. There are a huge variety of glues, including epoxy resins and super glues. All will have advantages and disadvantages and it is worth doing some research before you choose one. Do be aware that a lot of glues go yellow and brittle over time so, as with all projects, plan your design carefully to ensure it will be strong and wearable even if knocked. Consider having edges or posts inserted into items being attached to metal with glue to ensure they cannot be knocked off so easily.

Different Metals

All the previous step by step projects have focused on silver soldering processes that most jewellers will require when making jewellery or small metalsmithing items. Silver, copper, brass and gilding metal can be soldered in the same way using the same solder and flux. Other precious metals can also be soldered with silver solder, however this will affect the purity of the metal, which in turn may affect the hallmarking and aesthetics of the piece. This section covers a few differences that you may encounter when you start to experiment and explore other metals.

Silver

There are various qualities of silver and they are named differently in relation to the quantity of silver contained in them. The most commonly used silver for jewellery is sterling silver; this contains 92.5 per cent or more silver. Fine silver has 99 per cent or more silver content and is used less often for jewellery as it is softer, which can

Key Piece by Dauvit Alexander.
(Photo: Andrew Neilson, Neilson Photography)

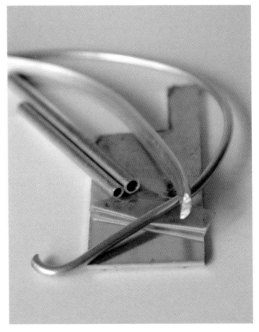

Silver tube, wire and sheet.

create pieces that can be damaged or bent easily. However, fine silver does have an advantage when making larger scale items and silversmithing as it can be repeatedly worked and heated without creating fire stain and allows a lot of work hardening to take place before it needs to be annealed in comparison to sterling silver. Other more recently developed silvers, such as Britannia silver and Argentium, have a higher silver content than sterling silver and lower silver content than fine silver. This was to create a silver with a balance of strength, malleability and a material that is less likely to get fire stain.

All these silvers are soldered and joined using the same processes as described in the projects in this book. The different silvers can be successfully soldered together without any problems.

Gold

Gold is rarely used in its pure form as it is extremely soft and will not withstand the wear and tear that everyday jewellery will go through. Pure gold is also known as twenty-four carat gold and, like silver, gold is alloyed with other metals to produce a harder material. Nine carat gold is only 37.5 per cent gold, fourteen carat is 58.3 per cent gold and eighteen carat is 75 per cent gold. Each gold is mixed with

Gold, sheet, tube and wire.

different alloys to create different colours, producing white gold, yellow gold, red or rose gold and even green gold.

Yellow gold is the most common and is mixed with silver, copper and zinc to create the varying carats. In the UK, gold is usually purchased in nine carat, eighteen carat or twenty-four carat and can be purchased from jewellery suppliers in the same forms as silver including tube, sheet, wire and in pre-made findings and fixings.

If you wish to solder gold and silver together it is best to use hard silver solder or easy gold solder to ensure you obtain a strong and secure joint. Other silver solders will not get hot enough to diffuse with the gold. You can also use silver solder to solder gold, but you may only choose to do this if you want to highlight the joints with a different colour as it will also affect the options of hallmarking the finished pieces.

Soldering gold is very similar to soldering silver. You need to ensure the surfaces that you wish to join fit well with no gaps and are clean from grease and dirt. The same flux can be used and the same surfaces and torches as explained earlier. A gold solder is used that melts at a lower temperature to the carat of gold the piece is being made from. If the metal and solder are heated to the right temperature the solder will be drawn into the joint and permeate the surface of the metal, giving it a strong and secure joint.

Jewellery suppliers sell gold solders, but in the form of panels and wire instead of strips like silver solder. Hard, medium and easy gold solders are manufactured for each carat of solder and all can be purchased in rose or red, yellow and white. Alternative forms for specialist processes can be purchased too; for example pastes and syringes that contain the solder and flux. Previously jewellers used gold that was two to four carats lower than the metal as a solder, but this can cause risk of not getting a colour match, the right melting temperature or the right quality for hallmarking.

Platinum and Palladium

Platinum is the most expensive of the precious metals. It has a high melting temperature and is extremely hard wearing. To get the required temperature to solder platinum together, the metal is usually welded using gas welding techniques or a micro welder and joined with platinum or platinum solder. Platinum is also resistant to corrosion and does not form an oxide layer so will not need to be fluxed or pickled.

Palladium is a lot less expensive than platinum, but like platinum is hard wearing, resistant to corrosion and requires welding techniques to join it. It is most commonly used in platinum solders and when adding to gold and silver alloys creates a hard, tarnish resistant surface called Rhodium plating.

When welding any materials remember to wear appropriate personal protective equipment. For welding, this will include specialist welding goggles or a shield, which have tinted or darkened lenses that will protect eyes from the light emitted at high temperatures.

Platinum rings by Rebecca Skeels.

Welding goggles. (H.S. Walsh and Son Ltd)

Ferrous Metals

Jewellers can choose from a variety of materials and metals, all of which have advantages and disadvantages and decisions of style, aesthetics and design as well as wearability and function. Most ferrous metals tarnish and corrode without treatment and are fairly heavy. However, careful consideration and experimentation can allow the jeweller to take advantage of these properties.

Stainless steel is a little different as it will not rust and patinate like other steels. It is used in the manufacture of products and architectural elements, but jewellers also use it regularly for tool making and in pins for brooches and fixings. Stainless steel is usually joined by welding or rivets, but can be soldered with silver solder or white gold solder to obtain the closest colour match.

Clean and prepare the metal by roughening the surface with emery paper. The seam must be really tight so the solder is drawn into the joint by capillary action. Flux the area with borax and use a high melting temperature solder such as enamel solder or hard solder. Heat the metal quickly and remove the heat as soon as the solder has flowed. As the flux is corrosive ensure it is removed completely by cleaning with an alkaline or bicarbonate of soda. Stainless steel is hard and unlikely to move through wear and tear. Do consult the section on basic edge to edge joints to see the options of making the joint stronger too.

Steel can also be welded using new laser and PUK techniques mentioned in Chapter One.

Pewter

Pewter is easily shaped and textured and is an ideal material to cast, however it is advisable to consider how the work is going to be worn. If the piece is knocked or rubs on another material it can be easily scratched.

Pewter is a very soft metal, mostly made up of tin, and is soldered with what is described in Chapter One as the soft solder process as it has a very low melting temperature. As well as soldering, pewter can be joined by welding and fusing. However, do take care as it can melt easily and the whole piece does not need to be heated as in hard soldering. Pointing the flame in one place for slightly too long can quickly create a hole or melt the entire piece. If purchasing pewter, make sure it is from a trusted supplier and is not lead-based. Pewter sold today does not contain lead. It is advisable not to wear or use lead as it can be harmful to health if it has contact with the skin or the fumes from heating it are inhaled.

When soldering pewter there are a variety of fluxes available and these are similar to those used when soldering circuit boards. Use a tin-based solder, but do make sure it does not contain lead for the same reasons mentioned in

**Yea Ha
by David Clarke.**

the previous paragraph. Use the same torch as you do for hard soldering, setting the flame to be soft and bushy or holding the torch a little further away than usual. Stick feeding works well or use pallions cut a little larger than usual. There is no need to pickle the metal afterwards, but do wash the piece thoroughly to ensure there are no remnants of flux left on the surface.

When working with pewter, make sure you use different tools and consumables to those you would with precious metals. If a small particle of pewter finds its way on to the silver, when the silver is heated a chemical reaction will cause a hole to emerge in the surface of the metal. This can have disastrous effects if it is not intended.

Aluminium

Aluminium is another white metal that has very different properties to the other metals. It can be welded, but usually only when making larger items. Smaller items, such as jewellery, are usually attached with rivets, tabs, stitches and other mechanisms.

Again, like pewter, avoid using the same tools and consumables that you would with precious metals as a small particle on silver will create a hole in the surface when it is heated.

One of the advantages of aluminium is that it can be anodized. This is a process that causes the pores on the surface of the metal to open and allow it to be dyed, then resealed to create a hard anodic layer on the surface, providing a large variety of colour choices to work with your designs.

Frog Brooch by Tom McDowell.
(Photo: Paul Hartley)

PROBLEM SOLVING

When something happens that you first think is an accident or problem take a moment to reflect on what was the outcome and, even though it was not what you were expecting, do you like it and does it do what you need it to do? The results are only problems if they are not giving a desired aesthetic and function.

Solder Not Flowing

Most problems are when solder does not flow and this is usually a result of rushing, a lack of planning or simply forgetting a step. The first checks are to ask yourself basic questions:

- **Did the pieces fit well together?**
- **Were they clean?**
- **Did you apply flux?**
- **Did you apply solder?**
- **Did you heat it enough?**
- **Did you clean your hands?**

When solder goes into a ball it is likely to be one or more of three things:

- **The metal is not heated enough and the solder is heated to melting temperature.**
- **The metal or solder is not clean.**
- **The solder is not in contact with the piece.**

OPPOSITE PAGE: **Melted silver.**

Not Enough or too Much Solder

Another common problem is either too much or not enough solder. This will become easier with practice and it is always worth erring on the side of too little rather than too much. If you have too little solder you can always add more, too much means you will need to clean and file the excess away, which is not only time consuming but may require more tools or tool making to get to hard to reach areas.

Fire Stain

If you regularly have problems with fire stain, the reddish purple blotch on the surface of silver, you are overheating your metal. Try to remove the heat as soon as the solder has flowed and the pieces have joined. On larger items you may wish to try a product called Argo-tect; this is specially made to prevent fire stain. Mix the powder with water and a tiny drop of washing up liquid to help it stick to the metal, then cover all surfaces of the metal that will be heated. This is not a guaranteed prevention, so try to keep to all the other rules too.

If you already have fire stain, some will only need a little extra sanding and polishing to remove it. If it is thicker, some jewellers acid dip their work. This is when the finished work is

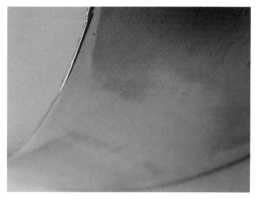

Fire stain on silver.

create a final even colour. There are a variety of options available depending on the company where you send your work. The last option is to oxidize your work, in which the surface of the silver is blackened. It is a very popular finish and gives a completely different feel and aesthetic.

The Metal Moves While Soldering

dipped in a very strong acid solution to remove a thin layer of the metal, but this is a dangerous process and it can also damage solder joints and leave a roughened surface.

The final options are really covering the problem of fire stain rather than removing it, but may suit the effect for which you are aiming. The fire stain can be thickened by reheating the final work to a bright red, being careful not to melt the solder, and pickling it. Do this five or six times, polish the metal lightly with rouge and leave an even layer of the fire stain. The work can also be plated with a thin layer of metal to

Remember that setting the work up for soldering is the main part of the process and this includes holding the work in place with tools or binding wire. Check that you have explored all the options available. If the pieces you are soldering together still move a lot during the process, it is likely that they are work-hardened and are trying to go back to their usual state as they are heated. Consider annealing the work before you solder it, ensure all edges are cleaned after you have annealed it and flux as normal.

If you have soldered the pieces together and they have moved and soldered in the wrong place,

Feather Series by Christine Johnson.

Earring post in the wrong place.

The post will come away as soon as the solder has melted.

Hold the post up a little while heating up the entire piece.

Keep heating and put the post in the correct position.

you have two options. The decision will depend on the size or length of the joint. If the joint is small, such as if an earring post is soldered in the wrong place, then the best option may be to move it.

Flux the joint and area where you wish to

Ends of a ring are not aligned.

Cut through the solder joint.

move the post. Set the earring on a soldering brick and hold it down with a home-made tool or a pair of tweezers, then with another pair of tweezers hold the earring and gently lift it as you warm the whole piece. When the solder has melted, the post will lift away completely, ready for you to clean and re-solder it in the desired position, or to place and solder in the correct position straight away.

If the solder joint is longer, for example the ends of a ring are not aligned, it is better to cut through the solder joint with a piercing saw, clean the area and then set up the work to be re-soldered.

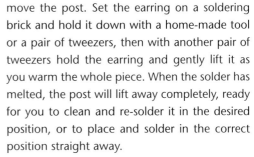

Set up and solder as before.

Re-soldered.

Holes

If you have created a hole in your work it will be difficult to fill with solder. A simple and effective method is to make the hole into a circle by enlarging it with a drill bit slightly bigger than the largest diameter of the mistake. Push a piece of round wire that is the same diameter as the drill bit into the drilled hole. Solder the wire in place, then cut and file to the surface of the original piece. This will be almost invisible once it is cleaned and finished, however you may wish to make a feature of this by putting a different colour metal in the hole. This will result in a coloured dot in the surface.

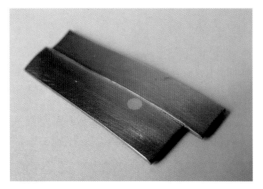

Drill and hole if there is a gap in your work and make a feature of it by soldering in a different coloured metal wire.

Conclusion and Observations

I hope this book goes some way in helping you understand and explore the soldering process, building your confidence and ambition.

The main aim of making your own work is to create something new and unique, so practise the soldering process as much as possible to enable you to tackle anything you wish to make. Start with soldering copper and gilding metal for the first few attempts of a new soldering technique and as soon as you have had one or two goes you will build your confidence and will be able to start on pieces of silver, gold, brass or whichever metal takes your fancy.

Remember you can change many design elements such as form, scale, textures, colours, weight, pattern, line and shape. This makes the options of what you can create endless, and you can draw inspiration from things you love and enjoy. Try out new ideas to see how you can push the boundaries and find new techniques and ways of doing things that suit you and create something that has never been done before. You will slowly find a method and style that you and many others appreciate and want.

The final stage is to wear your pieces out and about, show them off, talk about them and let them be admired.

FURTHER INFORMATION AND SUPPLIERS

Suppliers of Jewellery Tools, Jewellery Equipment, Jewellery Findings, and Materials

Alec Tiranti Ltd
Tiranti, 27 Warren Street, London, W1T 5NB,
United Kingdom
+44 (0)20 7380 0808
enquiries@tiranti.co.uk
www.tiranti.co.uk

Argex Limited
130 Hockley Hill, Hockley, Birmingham,
B18 5AN, United Kingdom
+44 (0)121 248 4344
silver@argex.co.uk
www.argex.co.uk

Bellore Rashbel
39 Greville Street, London, EC1N 8PJ,
United Kingdom
+44 (0)207 404 3220
orders@bellore.co.uk
www.rashbel.co.uk

Betts Metals
49–63, Spencer Street, Hockley, Birmingham,
B18 6DE, United Kingdom
+44 (0)121 233 2413
bms@bettsmetals.co.uk
www.bettsmetalsales.com

Cookson Precious Metals Ltd
Cooksongold, 49 Hatton Garden, London,
EC1N 8YS, United Kingdom
+44 (0)121 200 2120
info@cooksongold.com
www.cooksongold.com

Euro Mounts & Findings LLP
Antwerp House, 26–27 Kirby Street, Hatton
Garden, London, EC1N 8TE, United Kingdom
+44 (0)20 7404 5762
info@eurofindings.com
www.eurofindings.com

H.S. Walsh and Sons Ltd
Biggin Hill Head Office, Biggin Hill Airport,
Biggin Hill, Kent, TN16 3BN, United Kingdom
Hatton Garden Showrooms, 44 Hatton Garden,
London, EC1N 8ER, United Kingdom
Birmingham Showrooms, 1–2 Warstone Mews,
Birmingham, B18 6JB, United Kingdom
+44 (0)1959 543 660
mail@hswalsh.com
www.hswalsh.com

Johnson Matthey Metal Joining
York Way, Royston, Hertfordshire, SG8 5HJ,
United Kingdom
+44 (0)1763 253200
mj@matthey.com
www.jm-metaljoining.com

Kernowcraft Rocks & Gems Ltd
Penwartha Road, Bolingey, Perranporth,
Cornwall, TR6 0DH, United Kingdom
+44 (0)1872 573888
info@kernowcraft.com
www.kernowcraft.com

Lampert Werktechnik GmbH
Ettlebener Straße 27, 97440 Werneck,
Germany
+49 (0)97229459
mail@lampert.info
www.lampert.info

Rio Grande
7500 Bluewater Rd NW, Albuquerque, NM
87121, United States of America
+1 505.839.3011
www.riogrande.com

Suppliers of a Variety of Standard and Unusual Materials that Can Be Purchased in Small Quantities

Mindsets (UK) Ltd
Unit 10, The IO Centre,
Lea Road, Waltham Cross,
Herts, EN9 1AS, United Kingdom
+44 (0)1992 716 052
websales@mindsetsonline.co.uk
www.mindsetsonline.co.uk

Rapid Electronics Limited
sales@rapidonline.com
+44 (0)1206 751166
www.rapidonline.com

Assay Offices

Assay Office Birmingham
1 Moreton St, Birmingham,
B1 3AX, United Kingdom
+44 (0)121 236 6951
registration@theassayoffice.co.uk
www.theassayoffice.co.uk

Edinburgh Assay Office
Goldsmiths Hall, 24 Broughton Street,
Edinburgh, EH1 3RH, United Kingdom
+44 (0)131 556 1144
info@edinburghassayoffice.co.uk
www.edinburghassayoffice.co.uk

The Goldsmiths' Company Assay Office
Goldsmiths' Hall, Gutter Lane,
London, EC2V 8AQ, United Kingdom
+44 (0)20 7606 7010
www.thegoldsmiths.co.uk/craft/trade/assay-office

Sheffield Assay Office
Guardian's Hall, Beulah Road, Hillsborough,
Sheffield, S6 2AN, United Kingdom
+44 (0)114 231 2121
info@assayoffice.co.uk
www.assayoffice.co.uk

Organizations

Art Jewelry Forum
AJF, PO Box 823, Mill Valley,
CA 94942, United States of America
+1 415.860.5357
info@artjewelryforum.org
www.artjewelryforum.org

Crafts Council
44a Pentonville Road, Islington,
London, N1 9BY, United Kingdom
+44 (0)207 806 2500
reception@craftscouncil.org.uk
www.craftscouncil.org.uk

Goldsmiths' Company
Goldsmiths' Hall, Foster Lane,
London, EC2V 6BN, United Kingdom
+44 (0)20 7606 7010
the.clerk@thegoldsmiths.co.uk
www.thegoldsmiths.co.uk

The Goldsmiths' Centre
42 Britton Street, Clerkenwell,
London, EC1M 5AD, United Kingdom
+44 (0)20 7566 7650
info@goldsmiths-centre.org
www.goldsmiths-centre.org

Society of North American Goldsmiths
SNAG, PO Box 1355, Eugene,
OR 97440, United States of America
+1 541.345.5689
info@snagmetalsmith.org
www.snagmetalsmith.org

Health and Safety

Health and Safety Executive
www.hse.gov.uk

UKLPG
Camden House, Warwick Road, Kenilworth,
Warwickshire, CV8 1TH, United Kingdom
mail@uklpg.org
www.uklpg.org

World LPG Association
WLPGA, 182, avenue Charles de Gaulle,
92200 Neuilly-sur-Seine, France
+33 (0)1 78 99 13 30
association@wlpga.org
www.wlpga.org

Insurance

Hencilla Canworth Ltd.
Simpson House, 6 Cherry Orchard Road,
Croydon, CR9 6AZ, United Kingdom
+44 (0)20 8686 5050
mail@hencilla.co.uk
www.hencilla.co.uk

T.H. March
National Service Centre, Hare Park House,
Yelverton Business Park, Yelverton,
Devon, PL20 7LS, United Kingdom
+44 (0)1822 855555
insurance@thmarch.co.uk
www.thmarch.co.uk

More Information on the Author and Featured Artists

Dauvit Alexander
justified.sinner@gmail.com
www.justified-sinner.com

David Clarke
www.misterclarke.wordpress.com

Christine Johnson
www.christinejohnsonjewellery.com

Leigh Leal
info@leighleal.com
www.leighleal.com

Tom McDowell
+44 (0)7973 770 691
info@TomMcDowellDesign.com
www.TomMcDowellDesign.com

Rebecca Skeels
+44 (0)771 509 3690
Rebecca@skeels.co.uk
www.skeels.co.uk

Further Reading

The Theory and Practice of Goldsmithing,
by Professor Dr Erhard Brepohl.
(Brynmorgen Press, 2001).

*Introduction to Precious Metals – Metallurgy
for Jewelers & Silversmiths*, Mark Grimwade.
(Brynmorgen Press, 2009).

Jewelry Concepts and Technology,
Oppi Untracht.
(Robert Hale Ltd, 1985).

Pewter Studio, Lisa Slovis Mandel.
(Lark, 2010).

Websites and Forums

At the Bench
www.atthebench.com

a-n Artists Information Company
www.a-n.co.uk

Benchpeg
www.benchpeg.com

Crafthaus
www.crafthaus.ning.com

The Ganoksin Project
www.ganoksin.com

INDEX